A–Z

OF

PORTSMOUTH

PLACES - PEOPLE - HISTORY

Philip MacDougall

AMBERLEY

For Alec Dennis Jones (1920–2018), who, whilst in the Royal Artillery, helped defend Portsmouth during the Blitz.

First published 2018

Amberley Publishing
The Hill, Stroud, Gloucestershire, GL5 4EP
www.amberley-books.com

Copyright © Philip MacDougall, 2018

The right of Philip MacDougall to be identified as the Author of this work has been asserted in accordance with the Copyrights, Designs and Patents Act 1988.

ISBN 978 1 4456 8179 5 (print)
ISBN 978 1 4456 8180 1 (ebook)

British Library Cataloguing in Publication Data. A catalogue record for this book is available from the British Library.

Origination by Amberley Publishing.
Printed in Great Britain.

Contents

Introduction

A–Z of Portsmouth is designed to serve as a quick and convenient way of delving into the city's history. Through adopting an alphabetical approach, it permits the easy finding of various aspects of Portsmouth's history, rather than the reader having to wade through a book taking a more conventional chronological approach. In places I have attempted to be more light-hearted, presenting Portsmouth in a sprightlier fashion. Something else I have attempted is to look at aspects of Portsmouth's history that are featured less in other books, rather than writing extensively on what is easily found elsewhere. So, there is less here on the dockyard but more on the city of Portsmouth in areas away from the dockyard. Fortunately, and fitting into these self-imposed parameters, I have been able to include some of my favourite authors, such as Olivia Manning, Percy Westerman and Neville Shute, all of whom have strong connections with Portsmouth.

One thing that will become clear in this A–Z guide is the huge amount of destruction inflicted upon the city during the bombing of the Second World War. Many structures that might otherwise have been included in this book were destroyed at that time. The raid carried out on the night of 10/11 January 1941 was especially severe, leading to the destruction of the Hippodrome (an early twentieth-century theatre), the Royal Garrison Church, the Guildhall, Clarence Pier, the George Hotel (where Nelson ate his last breakfast on dry land) and numerous shops and houses in Commercial Road and the High Street. Frequent references are made to this raid, through mention of some of the buildings destroyed or what came to replace them. Especially sad is a memorial to fourteen victims all killed in this raid when a bomb destroyed the house in which they were living (No. 101 High Street). The memorial is to be found on the south-east side of the Anglican cathedral where that same house had once stood.

No other period in Portsmouth's history has seen such destruction. Instead the general theme has been one of growth and development. In the sixteenth century much of Portsea Island was given over to agriculture, the town of Portsmouth then occupying roughly that area of Portsea Island known today as 'Old Portsmouth'. From that time onwards, the number of people living on Portsea Island has grown continuously and often at a dramatic rate. Much of this early growth was dockyard related, as an increasing number of houses was required to accommodate those employed within its walls. As the yard expanded and the navy became increasingly dependent on its services, other facilities were created, these to provide a better defence from enemy attack, barracks for the billeting of soldiers and buildings for the stowage of ships' victuals and guns. In turn, this brought into Portsmouth those who were required to serve the needs of that increased naval, military and civil shipbuilding population, with Portsmouth eventually becoming one of the most densely packed of European cities.

Portsmouth from the air during the summer of 2005 with the naval base in the foreground. (MoD/Crown copyright, 2005)

To assist in the use of this book, rather than an index, cross-referencing has been introduced using bold text. Where an entry refers to a second subject found elsewhere in the book, this second topic appears in bold type, allowing the reader to quickly turn to this related entry where further information is provided.

A

Aerodrome

Believe it or not, Portsmouth once had its own aerodrome. This was located between Hilsea railway station and the Eastern Road, providing easy access into the centre of the city. Nowadays, Anchorage Park covers part of the former airfield together with several industrial and retail businesses. Officially opened on 2 July 1932, it was a project driven through by Portsmouth City **Corporation**, helped by grants from the government tied into construction of the aerodrome, bringing jobs to the local unemployed. Spreading over an area of 275 acres, the airport quickly gained a regular flight to Jersey while Airspeed, an aircraft manufacturing company, was also established on the aerodrome. Taken over by the Air Ministry during the war, civil flying returned upon the cessation of hostilities, with the Channel Islands continuing as a popular destination. The aerodrome, never given a tarmac runway, struggled

RAF aircraft arriving at Portsmouth Aerodrome where they will perform an aerial display to mark the official opening on 2 July 1932.

The V&A in Albert Road, a one-time police station.

to attract any large-scale commercial development, a situation made worse on 15 August 1967 when, following heavy rain, two Avro turbo-prop 748 airliners, both owned by Channel Air and within ninety minutes of each other, in attempting to land on the grass, skidded through the boundary fence, with one completely blocking the Eastern Road. Fortunately, no one was seriously injured, but the two incidents really marked the beginning of the end, with final closure of the aerodrome coming at the end of 1973.

Albert Road

If you are looking for a unique shopping experience, one that excludes retail chains and large department stores, then look no further than Albert Road. Running through the heart of Southsea, and almost ¾ of a mile in length, the road is a paradise of small shops and cafés with retailers specialising in everything from retro clothes and antique books through to furnishings and artwork. Many of the pubs – and there's no shortage of them – cater for real-ale fans, with the buildings often boasting an interesting and unusual history, not least the Goose at the V&A. With live music, real ale, darts and bar snacks, the V&A was once the Fuzz and Firkin, named due to the building having once been the local police station. Also in Albert Road is the recently restored King's Theatre and the Wedgewood Rooms, a live music and concert venue.

Portsmouth has always been closely connected with the Andrew, the Royal Navy, but not as close as might appear from this photograph of an impressive model battleship constructed to mark the coronation of George VI in May 1937.

The Andrew

A nickname for the Royal Navy, the origin of the term is obscure. Portsmouth, the home of the Royal Navy, has had a continuous connection with the service since 1495 when Henry VII built the first dry dock here. Through the navy being much reduced in size, the Admiralty is no longer the largest single employer in the city, but several **stone frigates** or naval establishments on land still exist in Portsmouth, these including HMS *Nelson* (the naval base), HMS *Excellent* (**Whale Island**) and HMS *Temeraire* (Burnaby Road).

Blitz and Pieces

With the naval dockyard serving as a major target for Luftwaffe bombers during the Second World War, Portsmouth, quite literally, was 'blitzed' to pieces. Outside of London, Portsmouth was one of the most heavily bombed areas in the country, with three especially massive raids occurring on the nights of 24 August 1940, 10 January and 10 March 1941. The official given total of raids to hit the city was sixty-seven, these all taking place between July 1940 and May 1944. In all, a total of 1,320 high-explosive bombs and 38,000 incendiary bombs were recorded as falling on the city, with 930 civilians killed and a further 2,837 injured. Many of those fatalities and injuries could have been avoided if the city had been better prepared during the years leading up to the war. The raid on the night of 10/11 January 1941 was especially destructive, resulting in Portsmouth losing many historic or otherwise important

In Old Portsmouth is this memorial to one of the many tragedies resulting from the wartime Blitz on the city.

George VI and Queen Elizabeth visiting bombed-out Commercial Road on 6 February 1941.

buildings, including one of Portsmouth's **theatres**, the Hippodrome, as well as the **Royal Garrison Church**, the **Guildhall**, **Clarence Pier** and the **George Hotel**. The **Corporation,** in its role of establishing an effective Air Raid Precaution (ARP) system, fell behind other towns and cities in the country, only appointing a committee to consider the matter in January 1937. Something that could have been done much earlier was the digging of tunnels into the chalk slope ridges of **Portsdown Hill**. It was only in June 1941 that the city's War Emergency Committee sanctioned the digging of tunnels and, once completed, they would provide sufficient room to accommodate over 3,000. Until that time, many of those living in the city felt forced to flee each night into the surrounding countryside, resulting in considerable anger. Many others were relying on hastily erected surface shelters that had been constructed in areas of poorer housing where garden Anderson shelters were impracticable. It was this sense of anger that was captured by the Mass Observation organisation during a series of interviews carried out in Portsmouth during the summer of 1941, with one fifty-five-year-old female dockyard worker complaining, 'they're still building them [the deep shelters]. But what I say is why didn't they do all that sort of thing before the war. They knew we was going to be bombed, didn't they?' And she was correct, they certainly did know that Portsmouth was going to be bombed.

One of several blue plaques to be found across the area of the city, this on the Portsmouth Grammar School building in Cambridge Road.

Blue Plaques

Portsmouth has nearly forty plaques, most of them blue plaques, commemorating famous individuals who have connections with Portsmouth, marking a place associated with that individual. One plaque, for instance, is to be found at No. 96 Castle Road, proclaiming the flat above to be where the actor Peter Sellers was born and another at No. 12 Helena Road where Commodore Edward Unwin, a recipient of the Victoria Cross, once lived. Other blue plaques mark the former homes of **Charles Dickens**, **Arthur Conan Doyle**, **Fred T. Jane**, **Rudyard Kipling**, **Neville Shute** Norway, **Thomas Ellis Owen**, **Percy F. Westerman** and two of the 'Cockleshell Heroes'.

Brunel, Marc

Marc Brunel, with his strong connections to Portsmouth, needs to be much better remembered than he is. He is frequently overshadowed by his son, Isambard Kingdom Brunel, the architect of both the *Great Eastern* steamship and Great Western Railway. As far as Portsmouth is concerned, the birth of Isambard can hardly be forgotten, with a major thoroughfare, a primary school and several buildings named either after him or his works; his father is largely forgotten. Marc Brunel was the designer of a revolutionary block mill in Portsmouth Dockyard that introduced, during the first decade of the nineteenth century, the concept of mass production using machinery, so saving the British government huge sums of money. Later he went on to design an equally innovative wood mill for the naval dockyard at Chatham. His most famous contribution to the world of engineering was the first Thames tunnel. One other of his inventions should not pass unmentioned, this being a machine for

The Block Mill, a massively important addition to the dockyard, with the machinery once used to mass produce naval blocks designed by Marc Brunel.

Marc Brunel, a man in need of much greater local recognition.

Despite Marc Brunel's contributions to Portsmouth, it is his son, Isambard Kingdom Brunel, who always gets the by-line.

manufacturing boots. He designed it in Portsmouth after witnessing the terrible state of footwear of troops returning from the Battle of Corunna. Marc, who was born in France, came to this country as an asylum seeker fleeing for his life from a Revolutionary government at war with Britain. Isambard was born in Britain Street on 9 April 1806. Despite Marc Brunel's significant contribution to the local military-industrial complex, the Admiralty never let him forget that he was an alien born in an enemy country, forcing him to produce an identity pass every time he entered the dockyard in connection with the block mill he had designed while all others passed into the yard on a simple nod of the head.

C

Camber

The Camber was the original port serving the town, camber a little-used term for a port or dockyard. Protected by the spit of land out of which **Spice Island** was created, the Camber supported the maritime commercial needs of the town, but with the expansion of these facilities restricted through being surrounded by various government facilities that included the **royal dockyard**, **Gunwharf** and fortifications. The town quay, where ships were unloaded, was positioned on the east side of the Inner Camber with entry into the town by way of one of the **town gates**, Quay Gate (later **King George's Gate**), which led directly onto the quay from the town of Portsmouth.

The Inner Camber by night.

A pleasant summer's day boating on Canoe Lake – 1950s style.

Canoe Lake

When first opened in 1886, Canoe Lake met with a certain degree of derision. Some accused Portsmouth **Corporation** of wasting rate payers' money, for while much had been spent on excluding a portion of Southsea Common from the sea through the building of a sea wall, 'the wiseacres of Portsmouth Council', it was claimed by the Portsmouth *Evening News*, 'have set to work to bring it back again in the shape of Canoe Lake'. Nevertheless, from the very beginning it proved a popular attraction, a man-made boating pond that each summer is crowded with cheaply hired pedal boats. To this, of course, can be added the attractive floral beddings to the south of the lake, a small café that opens all-year round and a children's play area. Personally, I prefer Canoe Lake in winter, which is seemingly more crowded, but not with humans: as many as sixty juvenile swans will descend upon you at the slightest rustle of a paper bag. I'm advised that bread can be harmful to the swans as it is difficult to digest, so it's always best to bring, or purchase from the Canoe Lake Café, wheat grain, which is much healthier for these friendly but sometimes persistent waterbirds.

Cathedral: Times Two

While unusual, Portsmouth is far from the only city in the UK with more than one cathedral. The earlier of the city's two cathedrals, if not in the age of the building, is the Roman Catholic Cathedral Church of St John the Evangelist in Edinburgh Road. Constructed during the latter years of the nineteenth century, with a foundation stone laid in 1880, the building is of red brick in Flemish bond with Portland stone dressings. Its style of architecture is medieval, and decorated with interior pointed arched

The medieval nave of the Anglican cathedral of St Thomas in Old Portsmouth.

Interior arched arcades and clustered columns of Portsmouth's Roman Catholic cathedral.

arcades and clustered columns with decorative leafy capitals. In Old Portsmouth is the Anglican cathedral, and while a medieval building dating in origin to the twelfth century, it only achieved cathedral status in 1927. Both buildings are worth visiting, St John's to see the lavish splendour of a Victorian church – and especially its wooden vaulted ceiling – and the cathedral of St Thomas for its fusion of several styles during past periods of rebuilding.

Cinemas

During the height of picture-going in the 1930s, Portsmouth had more than thirty cinemas. However only a few of the original buildings remain. This is one of

The Vue at Gunwharf Quays offers a very different film-going experience to those early cinemas that once dominated evening entertainment in Portsmouth.

Portsmouth's great losses, as many were unique in style, often quite palatial and very much a reflection of the age in which they were built. Of those buildings that remain, the exterior of the former Shaftsbury Cinema in Kingston Road is a personal favourite. First opened in the years before the First World War, it has an ornate and colourful façade, with the building having gone the way of many cinemas, that of becoming a bingo club. Also not to be missed is the former Majestic Picture House of 1921 in Kingston Road, the former Ambassador (later Odeon) in Cosham High Street (now Crown Bingo) opened in March 1937 and the former Odeon of 1936 (now Sainsbury's) in London Road.

Cockleshell Heroes

The 'Cockleshell Heroes' were members of a covert naval operation carried out in December 1942 that saw the placing of limpet mines on the hulls of enemy ships in Bordeaux. All were Royal Marines based in Portsmouth, with much of the training in preparation for the operation taking place in and around the former Royal Marine Barracks at **Eastney**. To get to Bordeaux, five two-man canoes (known as 'cockles', and from their use came the epithet 'cockleshell heroes') were rowed 70 miles up the River Gironde over a period of five nights, the party of ten having

Above left: The entrance to the Rose Garden has a memorial to the 'Cockleshell Heroes', for it was here, formerly the site of Lumps Fort, that the 'Cockleshell Heroes' trained.

Above right: Several other memorials are to be found in Southsea commemorating the 'Cockleshell Heroes' including one provided by Portsmouth City Council and unveiled on 6 July 1992 by Marine Bill Sparks DSM, one of the two 'Cockleshell Heroes' who survived the raid.

first taken to the French coast by submarine. A sixth canoe manned by two men was damaged while being unshipped, so reducing the original plan from a twelve-man party to that of ten. Ultimately, only two canoes got through to Bordeaux, but the raiding party was successful in sinking one ship and damaging others with use of the port severely disrupted for several months. Of the ten who had set out from the submarine, six were executed by the Nazis as saboteurs, two were presumed drowned and two, with the help of the French Resistance, returned to Portsmouth. To disguise the reason behind their training in the use of canoes, those who were to carry out the raid on Bordeaux were officially designated the Royal Marine Boom Patrol Detachment – viewed as the forerunners of the Special Boat Service (SBS).

Commercial Road

Commercial Road is Portsmouth's main shopping centre where most major chain stores are to be found. That it has a modern feel to it is the result of Commercial Road having to be completely rebuilt after the Second World War after most of the existing shops and buildings were destroyed by aerial bombing.

Commercial Road with Christmas approaching.

Corporation of Portsmouth

The Corporation was the governing body of Portsmouth prior to the local government reforms of the 1970s. In its original arrangement, prior to 1835, the Corporation was a self-perpetuating elite of individuals who ran the town very much to their own benefit. At that time, the Corporation governed only the town of Portsmouth and its immediate environs, with **Portsea** falling under the parish vestry. Reforms introduced in 1835 saw Portsmouth and Portsea falling under one authority. This authority also had extensive powers and, apart from also including police (and a fire brigade that was part of the police service), was not so dissimilar from the present-day unitary authority. While combining Portsmouth and Portsea, it was not until 1904 that Portsea Island, in its entirety, was brought into the borough, with Cosham added in 1920 and parts of Farlington and Portchester added in 1932.

Cosham

At the time of the **Domesday Book** Cosham was a tiny hamlet, part of the manor of Wymering. It was only during the nineteenth century that Cosham came of size, aided by the coming of the railway. It was not until 1920 that Cosham, which lies outside Portsea Island, became part of Portsmouth.

Aerial view of Cosham, *c.* 1930. This was a period of expansion for Cosham, many residents of Portsea Island choosing to relocate to Cosham at this time.

The original and still extant railway station at Cosham, Victorian but much altered and restored.

D-Day

Heavily bombed during the earlier years of the Second World War, D-Day, for Portsmouth, was payback time. The role of the city and the surrounding area was pivotal to the success of the landings, with Admiral Sir Bertram Ramsay, commander of the naval forces, saying 'the main burden of the operation, on the naval side, was perforce borne by the Portsmouth Command'. In Portsmouth Harbour, Spithead and the wider waters of the Solent, warships, coasters, lighters, tankers, tugs and every other sort of craft were crammed together, waiting to push forward into the Channel in support of the thousands of troops who would be landing on the beaches. Many of those troops had also been accommodated in Portsmouth during the preceding months, with Portsea Island having the appearance of one massive armed camp.

In June 1984, to mark the fortieth anniversary of D-Day, Queen Elizabeth The Queen Mother opened the D-Day Museum at Portsmouth, which was designed to tell the story of D-Day and the role of Portsmouth. More recently, the museum has seen, with the help of the Heritage Lottery Fund, a £4.9m refurbishment, with the museum reopened in the spring of 2018 with completely new displays using the stories of those who took part. Immediately outside the museum is a statue of Field Marshal Bernard Montgomery, a former Portsmouth Garrison commander who commanded the allied forces on D-Day and during the Normandy campaign.

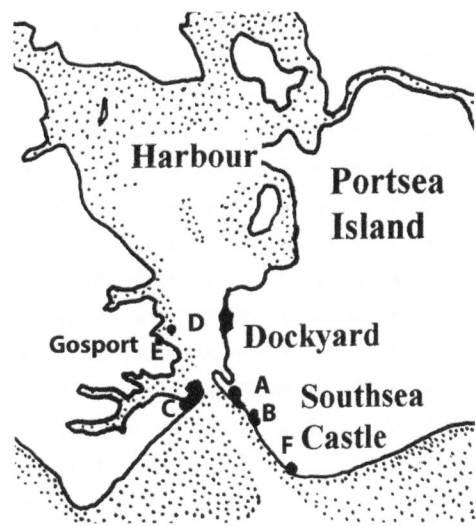

The location of the improvements made to Portsmouth's defences by Bernard de Gomme, these including the 'L' shaped battery adjacent to the Round Tower (A), Spur Redoubt and Curtain Wall (B), a 21-gun battery (C), Fort James (D) and Fort Charles (E) in the harbour and alterations to Southsea Castle (F).

de Gomme, Sir Bernard

Of Flemish descent, de Gomme was the Chief Engineer under Charles II from 1661 until 1685, instructed to commence a programme of renewing fortifications in England during the time of the Dutch Wars. The need to radically improve the existing fortifications protecting both the town of Portsmouth and its important naval dockyard became especially important following the Dutch raid on the Medway in 1667 in which the objective had been to destroy Sheerness and Chatham dockyards. Fear of a raid on Portsmouth led de Gomme to introduce several new features to the defence of the harbour, which included an 18-gun 'L' shaped battery adjacent to the **Round Tower**, alterations to **Southsea Castle** and the Long Curtain Wall and King's Bastion to the south-east of Garrison church. On completion, and including defence structures predating de Gomme, this made Portsmouth one of the most fortified towns in the whole kingdom.

Dickens, Charles

Charles Dickens was born in Portsmouth on 7 February 1812 at No. 1 Mile End Terrace in Portsea (now No. 393 Old Commercial Road). This house is now a museum and is marked by a blue plaque. Unfortunately, other places associated with Dickens during the early years of his life, and before a move to Chatham, have mostly disappeared. He was baptised on 4 March 1812, in the medieval font of Portsea Parish Church, a building destroyed by bombing during the Second World War, although the baptismal font survives at St Alban's Church, Copnor Road. The family later moved to No. 16 Hawk Street, a white plaque in Hawk Street marking this connection. This house no longer survives, nor does a third family home at No. 38 Wish Street in Southsea. His father, John Dickens, was a naval pay clerk who worked in the dockyard. A third memorial

Statue in Guildhall Square memorializing Charles Dickens, who was born in Portsmouth.

plaque to Dickens is to be found in Southsea Terrace and relates to his stay at the Pier Hotel in May 1866, the author on the 24th and 25th of that month giving readings in St George's Hall, St George's Square. Again, this is another lost site. The grave of Ellen Ternan, actress and the author's mistress, can be found in the Highland Road Cemetery.

Dreadnought

Launched at the dockyard on 10 February 1906, HMS *Dreadnought* was a revolution in battleship design. Not only was she appreciably larger than any previously built battleship, but she was the first powered by steam turbines and fitted only with big-gun armament. Through the introduction of steam turbines she was, at the time of her completion, the fastest battleship in the world, while the dispensing of secondary armament made her the most heavily armed warship at the time of her commissioning, carrying ten 12-inch guns. She made all previous battleships effectively obsolete, with her name becoming a generic term for a modern battleship – all battleships built during the previous thirty years became known as 'pre-dreadnoughts'. In the years that followed her launch, Portsmouth continued to build battleships, launching a new and larger dreadnought in each of the years leading up to the outbreak of the First World War.

Dreadnought leaving Portsmouth Harbour.

Domesday Book

Now one of the most densely packed cities in Europe, with a population over 200,000, in 1087, at the time of the Domesday Book, the population of the present-day Portsmouth city area was probably less than 300. Portsmouth doesn't get a mention, but manors that can be identified as part of the area of the present-day unitary authority are Buckland (Bocheland), Copnor (Copenore), Fratton (Froddington), Cosham (Coseham) and Wymering (Wineringes).

Doyle, Sir Arthur Conan

Sir Arthur Conan Doyle, the author of the Sherlock Holmes detective fiction, lived at No. 1 Bush Villas in Southsea from 1882 until 1890 where he was a medical doctor. It was here that his first Sherlock Holmes novel, *A Study in Scarlet*, was written. A blue plaque marking the site of No. 1 Bush Villas, his former home, which was destroyed by bombing during the war, is to be found in Elm Grove. More about Conan Doyle and his connections with Portsmouth can be found in Portsmouth Museum, which has a dedicated display to the author and his works.

Dolling, Father Robert

Father Robert Dolling is one of those lesser-known names in Portsmouth, but one that should be better known. A Roman Catholic priest born in County Down, he led a mission into Landport, the most impoverished area of Portsmouth during the late nineteenth century and at the time dominated by Irish-born settlers. Using money that he helped raise he opened several schools, converted a disused Baptist chapel into a gymnasium and organised activities for the poor. His crowning achievement is St Agatha's Church in Landport, which today serves Anglicans who wish to draw nearer to the Roman Catholic Church.

St Agatha's Church in Landport.

Eastney

On the south-east corner of Portsmouth, Eastney was at one time dominated by the Royal Marines through the presence of **Eastney Barracks**, built between 1862 and 1867 for the Royal Marine Artillery. Part of the beach at Eastney serves as an unofficial naturist site while at the extreme east end of Eastney, just past **Fort Cumberland** and **Eastney Beam Engine House**, a small ferry operates a regular daily service to Hayling Island.

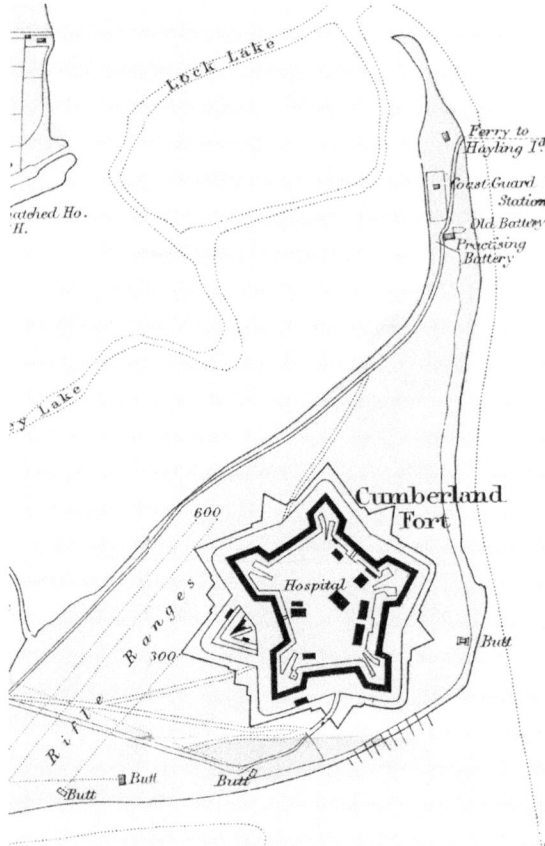

A map of Eastney showing the outline of Fort Cumberland when it was occupied by the Royal Marine Artillery and used for training. Nearby is the boarding point for the Hayling Island ferry.

Eastney Barracks

In 1923, upon the amalgamation of the Royal Marine Light Infantry and the Royal Marine Artillery, Eastney became home of the Portsmouth Division. It was here that the Royal Marine Boom Patrol Detachment, better known as the '**Cockleshell Heroes**', were based

Above: With Eastney Barracks in the background, the Royal Marine Artillery are seen marching to church.

Below: The Parade Ground, Eastney Barracks.

The Barracks today with just one remaining Royal Marine.

and set out for the raid on Bordeaux. Today, the barracks, while still an impressive reminder of times past, following its closure in 1991 has now been redeveloped for housing. The Royal Marine Museum, which remained within the site of the former barracks until April 2017, is now closed and is in the process of moving to Portsmouth **Historic Dockyard** where it will reopen in 2020 as a state-of-the-art museum occupying an original Victorian boathouse close to the Victory Gate visitor's entrance.

Eastney Beam Engine House

The Eastney Beam Engine House, a Grade II-listed building, is in Henderson Road. Periodically made open to the public by Portsmouth Museum, it is a magnificent Victorian building that houses a pair of Boulton Watt beam engines and pumps dating to 1887. Designed by Sir Frederick Bramwell, its purpose was the pumping of sewage into the sea.

Electric Trams

An early morning commute across Portsmouth to the dockyard by tram could be made at the special workers' rate of one penny. This was cheap, but not the most comfortable of experiences, especially if the tram was crowded and the only available seats were on the open-top upper deck; maybe reasonably pleasant during the height of summer but a fearful experience in the midst of winter, especially route 13, which passed along the

Portsmouth's last electric tram, 10 November 1936.

seafront, the upper deck exposed to every blast of freezing wind-driven rain. Mind you, the lower deck was none too pleasant with its wooden benches and rooves that often leaked, letting rainwater fall onto passengers huddled together to keep warm. This, of course, would be a daily experience for many, or at least until the open-top trams were replaced by **trolleybuses**. Incidentally, the one-penny fare was for workers and only available before 08.45 a.m. with a return fare of two pennies. At all other times of the day fares were four times this amount. It was in 1901 that electric trams first arrived in Portsmouth, the opening ceremony on 21 September seeing a certain Mrs Kimber, the wife of the chairman of the Corporation Tramway Committee, tentatively driving Tram No. 1 a short distance under the watchful gaze of a newly recruited senior driver. All had been made possible by the **Corporation** having decided that it would create a network of electric tram routes across the city, taking over the company that had previously operated the **horse trams** so that the rails previously laid would now be used by electric trams. Electric trams were to continue running in Portsmouth until 1936. Providing the necessary power was a purpose-built generating station in Vivash Road, electricity distributed throughout the various routes by cables linked to feeder poles. At its height, Portsmouth Corporation Tramways operated 114 tramcars, with the largest of these having seating capacity for fifty-five passengers.

Farlington Marshes Seaplane Base

In 1936, with Imperial Airways about to take delivery of twenty-eight luxury Short Brothers-built C-class Empire flying boats that were designed to whisk the wealthy and famous across the Atlantic along the length of Africa or to the Far East, Portsmouth **Corporation** came up with a plan that would have seen Farlington Marshes developed as the home base for these airliners that could seat around twenty, with the northern section of Langston Harbour used for taking off and landing. The proposal, which was still being pushed forward during the mid-1940s, would have required damming part of the harbour so that tidewater would be held at a constant level, creating an area of 5 square miles on which flying boats of any dimensions could alight in any weather. The hub of the seaplane base would be Langstone. Here jetties would project

If the seaplane station had been built at Langstone, then large flying boats, such as this Short C-Class Empire, would have been a regular sight flying into Portsmouth.

The area of Farlington Marshes, now a nature reserve, which was, at one time, seen as ideal for conversion into a seaplane base to be operated by Imperial Airways (later British Overseas Airways Corporation).

out into the water, similar to a ship harbour, while on the reclaimed marshland repair shops, hangars, the necessary passenger accommodation and a new **aerodrome** for landplanes would be built, with the land belonging to the existing aerodrome sold off for development. In all, it was supposed that this would bring permanent work for at least 3,000, with housing also to be provided in the Langston area to accommodate those employed on the base. At the time Portsmouth was one of three or four centres under consideration by Imperial Airways and the Air Ministry, with Southampton eventually winning out.

First Fleet

First Fleet is the name given to the eleven ships that departed Portsmouth on 13 May 1787 to establish a penal colony in Australia, this being the first European settlement in that land. Consisting of nine hired vessels and an escort of two naval ships, the First Fleet, under the command of Captain Arthur Phillip, took with it 759 convicts, of whom twenty-three died on passage. The voyage, which ended at Botany Bay, took eight months.

Portsmouth memorial to the First Fleet.

Fort Cumberland

The present-day Fort Cumberland was built between 1785 and 1812, replacing an earlier fort on the same site. Its purpose was to guard the entrance to Langstone Harbour, so preventing an enemy landing aimed at capturing or destroying the **royal dockyard.** In 1858, the fort was handed over to the Admiralty for occupation by the Royal Marine Artillery (RMA), whose main barracks were nearby. Here, the RMA took responsibility for manning a series of modern guns brought to the fort while also using the fort for training. Vacated by the Admiralty in 1971, it is now an archaeological centre and store for English Heritage.

G

Galley Arsenal

Although the present-day site of the naval dockyard at Portsmouth was established in the 1490s by Henry VII, an earlier royal dockyard also existed at Portsmouth on an area of foreshore that now lies inland and immediately north-west of the present-day **Gunwharf Quays**. This was built during the reign of Richard I to accommodate a fleet of galleys and enlarged and improved by King John. Although uncertainty exists as to its exact layout, it would almost certainly have consisted of an open area of water fronted by several timber sheds to house at least ten galleys together with additional workshops and storehouses. Abandoned during the reign of Henry III, it seems he ordered the walls of the arsenal to be demolished in 1253 and the stone reused to repair his town house. The approximate site of Portsmouth's first **royal dockyard** is nowadays marked by an information board located alongside Ordnance Row and not far from St George's Church.

George Hotel

It was at the George Hotel in the High Street that Admiral Lord **Nelson** took breakfast on 14 September 1805 before leaving Portsmouth for his eventual meeting with the combined French and Spanish fleet at Trafalgar. The hotel was destroyed in the bombing **Blitz** of 10 January, and the former site of the hotel is marked by an orientation board, which includes the information that not only did Nelson and other naval officers frequently stay at the George, but that Nelson's room was preserved as a tribute to him until the time of the hotel's destruction.

Guildhall

The Victorians loved ceremonies, pageants and street parades. In an age that offered little in the way of home entertainment, the public streets could often bring much-needed variety to the drudgery of everyday life. It's hard to imagine that Portsmouth today would come to a complete commercial standstill just to mark the opening of a new civic building, but that's exactly what happened when the Guildhall, an indisputably impressive building with its grand external staircase and portico and which was once topped by an also much more impressive clock tower replete with domes and cupolas, was officially opened on Saturday 9 August 1890 by the Prince of Wales (the future Edward VII). Prior to the day, the Mayor of Portsmouth, Sir William King, had called upon all places of business to shut down for the entire afternoon through to 6 p.m., allowing staff they employed to view the events of the day. On Southsea Common a huge assembly of local societies from Druids and stonemasons through to the Water Buffaloes and Sons of Phoenix had gathered prior to marching in procession through the main streets before arriving at the newly completed Guildhall, then referred to as the Town Hall. The Prince of Wales, of course, did not join that procession; he came into Portsmouth by way of the dockyard, proceeding along Queen Street and Edinburgh Road to arrive at the Town Hall at around 3 p.m. It was all an elaborate and carefully planned day, crowds lining the streets leading to the Guildhall, while in the evening massed bands gave a concert in Victoria Park and the navy an electric light display near the new Town Hall. Of course, the question must be raised, what happened to that much more impressive clock tower that once bedecked the present-day Guildhall? This, unfortunately, was a victim of wartime bombing, the building gutted on the inside by firebombs on the night of 10/11 January 1941. Although the exterior walls remained, the clock tower was substantially damaged and restored to a slightly altered design.

The original first Town Hall, the building that preceded the Guildhall, stood in the High Street and is seen here in an engraving dating to around the year 1820.

Right: The new Town Hall, later Guildhall, as it appeared shortly after its opening in 1890.

Below: The Guildhall today. Externally, it does differ in detail from the Guildhall built during the reign of Queen Victoria, having suffered extensive damage during the Blitz.

Gunwharf Quays

While now home, so the advertising claims, to over ninety premium retail outlet stores along with a nightclub, art gallery, cinema and casino, this area to shop until you drop once had a very different purpose to fulfil. Formerly an area of reclaimed

The Gunwharf Quays shopping centre.

In developing the former Gunwharf into a multi-functional centre for shopping, entertainment and housing, a mix of old and new have been carefully blended.

marshland, it first became a massive complex for the repair and storage of naval and army guns. During the seventeenth and eighteenth centuries, warships heading into the dockyard for repair or being held in the harbour would have their cannons and all other weapons shipped over to the Gunwharf where they would be removed and stored, to be returned when the ship was put back to sea. In time, the role of the Gunwharf as a place for storing ordnance declined and it was handed over to the Royal Navy as a shore establishment under the name HMS *Vernon*, specialising in mine warfare. Having been released by the navy in 1995, the former Gunwharf, renamed Gunwharf Quays, was opened in 2001 as a shopping centre. Under construction, Gunwharf Quays became central to one of **Graham Hurley's** locally based crime stories, the victim of a murder buried in the concrete of the foundations that were at that time being laid.

Handleys' Corner

Handleys' Corner was the name once given to the corner in Southsea formed by Palmerston and Osborne Roads. Here, until its destruction in the horrific air raid on the evening of 10 January 1941, stood the original Handleys department store, which was simply the place to be seen when shopping. Rebuilt after the war, it later became a branch of Debenhams.

One of
Southsea's Greatest
Attractions

IN Southsea, Handleys is recognized by residents and visitors alike as the premier Shopping Rendezvous.

The congenial atmosphere, bright and colourful merchandise always attractively displayed, make shopping at this delightful store more pleasant and less fatiguing.

There is no shop quite like Handleys

Established for seventy years, it stands as a monument to the Spirit of Progress and Industry and is not unworthy of a proud and historic city.

Handleys

FASHIONS
FURNISHINGS
RESTAURANT
HAIRDRESSING
MANS SHOP

Handleys Ltd., Palmerston Road, Southsea.   Telephone 224

A 1937 advertisement for 'one of Southsea's greatest attractions'.

An aerial view of the former Royal Dockyard, now HM Naval Base Portsmouth, as seen at the time when the 200th anniversary of Trafalgar was celebrated through the holding of a Fleet Review. The two ships berthed towards the centre are F89 Nigerian Frigate NNS *Aradu*, seen alongside PNS *Tipu Sultan* of the Pakistani navy. (MoD/Crown copyright, 2005)

Her Majesty's Naval Base (HMNB)

HM Naval Base Portsmouth is now the official name given to the operational facilities of the Royal Navy in Portsmouth including the now privatized repair and maintenance units that once formed part of the royal dockyard. Within the naval base there are fifteen stone-built docks, three large basins for the reception of ships and a complex of buildings dedicated to the refitting of naval warships that includes the recently named Vernon Complex, a primary centre for the navy's eight Hunt-class mine counter-measure vessels. The naval base will also be home to the new 'Queen Elizabeth'-class aircraft carriers, of which the name ship of that class, *Queen Elizabeth*, first berthed alongside the naval base in August 2017 with her commissioning ceremony performed by the Queen some three months later. To receive these ships, much preparation has been required, including significant dredging of the harbour, the laying of navigational aids and the rebuilding of the middle jetty as part of a centre of specialization that will house the engineers, logisticians and waterfront staff of 'Team Portsmouth'.

Hilsea Lido

First opened in July 1935, and developed at a cost of £40,000, Portsmouth Lido was once the place to be seen, with residents from all over Portsmouth drawn to its main pool, which could accommodate some 900 swimmers. Here, also, national diving championship competitions were once held, water spectaculars took place, and displays by the League of Health and Beauty were given. To view these events, the lido had seating for 1,000 spectators.

The Lido shortly after it
first opened in 1935.

Hilsea Lines

The Hilsea Lines, running along the northern shoreline of Portsea Island and following the natural course of the Hilsea Channel, was initially no more than a moated earthen rampart built during the mid-eighteenth century. In preventing incursions into Portsmouth, they were incredibly successful, as it was the existence of those early ramparts that fended off early plans for a railway, a planned line that was to be an extension of the one already connecting Chichester and Brighton. Undoubtedly, this must count as the greatest success of the Hilsea Lines in its perceived role of preventing invaders, if only tourists, from gaining entry onto Portsea Island. That success was short-lived, as in 1847 a railway line was cut through the ramparts, gaining access through a fortified short tunnel with a retractable drawbridge. In the late 1850s the earthen ramparts of Hilsea were completely remodelled, giving way to the much more solid brick structure that is visible today and which forms the backdrop to a publicly accessible nature reserve.

Now a nature reserve cared for
by the city council, this stretch
of water was part of the moat
that ran along the forward front
of the Hilsea Lines.

Expense Magazine on the Hilsea Lines, which was once used to store ammunition for the nearby guns. Heavily reinforced with a covering of chalk and earth, they were used as impromptu air-raid shelters during the Second World War.

Historic Dockyard

The Historic Dockyard, entered through Victory Gate (one time known as Main Gate), is the area of the former royal dockyard that is open to the public. It contains several historically interesting buildings, the museum of the Royal Navy and other attractions including *Mary Rose* (a Tudor navy flagship), *Victory* (Admiral Lord Nelson's flagship at Trafalgar), *Warrior* (the Royal Navy's first iron battleship) and *M.33* (a survivor of the Gallipoli campaign of 1915). While outside the immediate area accessible to the public, several other structures of historic interest are visible, these to be seen from the open area to the stern of *Victory*. The enclosed area of water to her immediate stern dates to the 1690s, its purpose that of allowing warships to be equipped more conveniently than in the open waters of the adjoining harbour. Originally known as the Great Basin, it was enlarged to the south between 1796 and 1805 and at this time was provided with two additional dry docks. On the far side of the basin are several structures from the Georgian period, including the building that housed the block mill designed by **Marc Brunel**.

Horse Buses

Horse buses, normally seating around twenty-six passengers on an upper and lower deck and drawn by two horses, began operating in Portsmouth in 1840. Until the arrival of **horse trams** in the 1860s, the horse bus represented the cheapest means of conveyance across the town on routes extending between residential areas, places of entertainment, shops and workplaces. The last horse bus service in Portsmouth was not phased out until 1920, this running on a route between Goldsmith Avenue and the **royal dockyard**.

Horse Trams

Horse-pulled trams had the advantage over horse buses of carrying a greater number of passengers but the disadvantage of being restricted to only those routes where rail lines had been built into the roadway. The first horse tram service in Portsmouth

The Hot Walls.

was opened in 1865 and ran from the town railway station to Clarence Pier and was primarily aimed at passengers crossing by ferry over to the Isle of Wight. Other routes were subsequently opened, with 14 miles of track eventually laid. It was the introduction of **electric trams** in 1901, using the same tracks as used by the horse trams, which marked the end of the horse tram in Portsmouth, although horse trams continued to operate a service between Hilsea Lines and Cosham until 1903.

Hot Walls

The Hot Walls stretch between the Square Tower and the **Round Tower** in Old Portsmouth and provide an ideal spot for sunbathing, the walls acting as a natural break from the winds while radiating the heat of the sun. Originally part of the earliest defences of the town, the Hot Walls date in part to the fifteenth century. Purchased from the War Office during the 1930s, this further opened Portsmouth as a resort for summertime visitors, giving the **Corporation** a hold on a beach now 2 miles long. More recently, the Hot Walls were subject to a £1.75m revamp that has brought a few small shops and a restaurant to this popular area of Portsmouth.

Hurley, Graham

With twelve novels to his name that feature Portsmouth-based detective Inspector Joe Faraday, these are books not to be missed by anyone with an interest in either Portsmouth or crime fiction. Faraday is a very real down-to-earth character with a house overlooking **Langstone Harbour** and who attempts to spend time out on **Farlington Marshes** one half-day a week. Hurley, in writing about Faraday, frequently alludes to the peace and solitude of the marshes, where Faraday is 'fascinated by the pageant of wildlife' that constantly unfolds 'on the wide, bright spaces of the harbour'. In turn, Hurley frequently contrasts this with the other side of Portsmouth, a Portsmouth of 'a hundred and fifty thousand people ... jigsawed together in street after street of terraced housing'. While none too flattering about the city, Hurley does present it very much as it is: 'impossible' traffic, 'non-existent' parking and pay rates 'often pitiable'.

Ice Cream *a la* Portsmouth

You couldn't get better ice cream anywhere than Portsmouth – at least this appears to have been the view of King George V. During a visit to Portsmouth in the early years of the twentieth century, the king apparently went into a local shop to purchase an ice cream. He then had this same shop regularly deliver ice cream to Buckingham Palace. The shop was that of Sabatino Pitassi's and was in Edinburgh Road, although that same shop today doesn't sell ice cream. Sabatino and his wife are still there, or rather two stone reliefs of their faces peering across Edinburgh Road from the first floor of the shop are. Sabatino, Italian by birth, came to Portsmouth with his brother Domenico sometime during the 1880s, with Sabatino selling ice cream from a handcart before he had enough money to invest in a shop. Domenico took up an alternative trade, as a craftsman in stone and marble, his business later taken over by his son Adolpho. Almost certainly, the two stone reliefs above the shop are a product of Domenico or his son, with other examples of their work to be found as decorative additions to several of Portsmouth's early cinemas.

Above left: Sabatino Pitassi, or rather a stone relief of his face, peers down onto the happenings of Edinburgh Road. The relief was almost certainly completed by his talented brother Domenico.

Above right: Domenico Pitassi also produced the exterior decorative artwork for a number of Portsmouth's early cinemas including this fine example still to be seen on the former Shaftsbury Cinema in North End.

J

Jack the Painter, aka James Aitken

Jack the Painter was hanged in public outside the main entrance to Portsmouth dockyard on Thursday 10 March 1777. His passion – independence for the United States of America. His crime – attempting to destroy British seaborne naval power. While no genius, James Aitken, often known as 'Jack the Painter' because he was a house painter, had come up with a solution as to how the small colony of America could defeat mighty Great Britain to achieve its independence. Quite simply, as Aitken realised, Britain's power lay with the navy. It was the Royal Navy that dominated the seas around America and it was the navy that escorted the ships that brought the soldiers that supported British power on land. Destroy the naval dockyards in England, starting with Portsmouth, and the Royal Navy would be greatly weakened. His way of destroying the dockyards was to burn them down using a small device he had specially made for him by a metalsmith in Canterbury. Once lit, this device, described by his enemies as an 'infernal machine', would, after a short while, shoot flames onto any nearby object. All he had to do was get into the dockyard at Portsmouth, secrete this 'infernal machine' into the hemp house, light, metaphorically, the blue touch paper and retire to another dockyard to repeat the exercise. In this he was successful, up to a point, managing with ease to get into the dockyard at Portsmouth overnight and carrying out his plan, but the fire that he created destroyed only part of the yard, the hemp house and much of the ropery. Some of the sparks spread to ships in dock, but none were destroyed, these fires put out by the dockyard workers who were urgently called into the yard by the ringing of the dockyard bell. James Aitken managed to escape but was caught in Bristol where he planned to set fire to several warehouses. Following a brief trial in Winchester – most trials were brief in those days – he was returned to Portsmouth and his appointment with the long drop.

Jane's *All the World's Fighting Ships*

Portsmouth being the home of the Royal Navy, it would be difficult not to include the city's connection with Frederick Thomas Jane, the founding editor of *All the World's Fighting Ships*, the definitive annual publication on the subject that was first published in 1898. It is still published alongside Janes' *All the World's Aircraft* and numerous other titles covering military, business and security issues. Jane spent most of his life at No. 17 Elphinstone Road in Southsea, a building marked with a blue plaque. He is buried in Highland Road cemetery. While living in Portsmouth he became heavily involved in politics, standing unsuccessfully as a parliamentary candidate. In 1910 his opponent was a Liberal and in coaxing a sailor to put forward a question at a public meeting, managed to persuade the Liberal candidate to give his support for the navy to be supplied with hammock ladders should he be elected.

John Pounds Memorial Church and Workshop

John Pounds, a shoemaker living in Portsmouth during the early eighteenth century, began teaching, in his own time, children of poor families who would otherwise not receive an education. Viewed as an inspiration for the Ragged School Movement, a

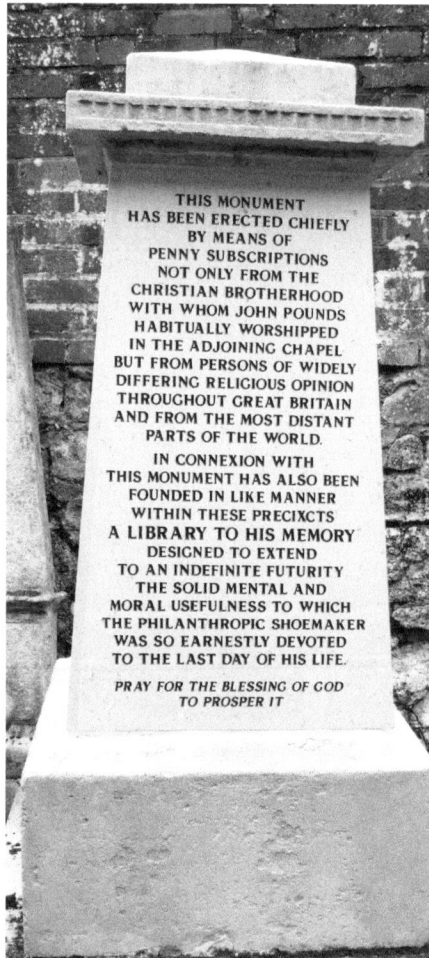

The John Pounds memorial can be seen close by a specially built memorial workshop in the High Street.

John Pounds' house, which originally stood in St Mary's Street but was destroyed by bombing during the Second World War, was painted by the artist W. L. **Wyllie** during the 1920s and formed part of a collection of his works depicting scenes in Old Portsmouth and Southsea.

national charity for the teaching of poor children, a memorial church and workshop commemorating John Pounds is to be found on the High Street. After his death in 1839, Pounds' work of educating the poor was continued in Portsmouth, a charitable group of mainly women opening a free school in his name for the poor in Kent Street. The Memorial Church and workshop, while not John Pounds' original workshop (this was in St Mary's Street and no longer exists), is on the site of the Unitarian chapel that Pound attended on Sundays. The original chapel was destroyed during the war, and the present chapel's foundation stone was laid on 24 September 1955.

Kangaroos

The Royal Navy was at the forefront of scientific exploration and discovery during the eighteenth century, with naval officers such as Cook, Bligh and Flinders sent out on scientific expeditions, these voyages usually starting and ending in Portsmouth. For instance, Matthew Flinders, commander of the sloop *Investigator*, left Portsmouth on 18 July 1801 to survey and chart the coastline of Australia, finally returning to Portsmouth in October 1810. Bligh set off in the *Bounty* from Portsmouth, bound for Tahiti, on 23 December 1787. Other naval ships, in having been sent into the Pacific or returning from Australia, brought with them strange cargoes, such as a kangaroo during the early years of the nineteenth century, the first example of this species ever brought to England – at the request of Britain's leading scientist Sir Joseph Banks. Nobody in Portsmouth knew how to look after such an exotic animal, so an expert from London, Philip Castang, was sent to Portsmouth to bring it to Sir Joseph in London. Philip Castang, my own great-great-great-great-uncle, had long been connected with the care of imported animals and frequently worked for Sir Joseph.

Memorial to Matthew Flinders located alongside the Square Tower on the landward side of the Hot Walls.

Kim

Kim is the title of a novel by Rudyard Kipling. Kim, the main character, is the orphan of an Irish soldier who lives an impoverished life in British India in the nineteenth century. Does the novel have a connection with Portsmouth? The answer is yes. Viewed by many as one of the great novels of the twentieth century, its writing was possibly stimulated by the author's unhappy childhood years spent in Southsea between October 1871 and April 1877. Here, he felt himself to be an outsider, for having spent the first five years of his life in India, he was brought back to England to be educated, living at Lorne Lodge in Southsea with a couple who boarded children for parents who were in India. For Rudyard this was a time of great unhappiness and in later life he said of Lorne Lodge, 'I should like to burn it down and plough the place with salt.' *Kim*, first serialised in magazine format at the turn of the century, may well reflect what life was like for the young Rudyard had he not been sent to Southsea to go through the suffering of being detached from his parents and living in a house where he was deprived of love. Admittedly, Kipling did not come from an impoverished family, but his time in Southsea was as if he had been orphaned and he would certainly have fantasized about life in India. Kipling himself makes a connection to Southsea with his entry into the world of fiction, and as explained in his brief autobiography, to survive in that house in Southsea as a child he frequently had to 'contradict himself' and maintain that contradiction into the following day. Adding, 'and this, I presume, is the foundation of literary effort'. As for Lorne Lodge, which is in Campbell Road, this is now marked by a blue plaque.

Kingston Prison

In 2013, Kingston Prison in Portsmouth had an open day – this might seem an unlikely event for a prison until it is realised that the prison had been closed earlier that same year. The open day was to allow local residents access inside those enclosing walls and to get some idea of what life had been like for those who had once been incarcerated within. Currently the site is under development for 230 new homes (157 flats and seventy-three family properties). Originally built in 1877, the prison was constructed on a radial design principal, the corridors of the prison branching out from a central hub and from where the inmates could be seen from a central observation point providing visual access to all wings.

Kipps

Kipps is a humorous novel written by Herbert George Wells and first published in 1905. It might not, at first glance, appear to have much of a connection with Portsmouth, the town not getting a single mention. But such an assumption would be wrong. Kipps, the main character, was a very unhappy draper's apprentice who eventually escaped from the drudgery of the drapery store by way of unexpected inheritance. How like Wells' own early experiences of life when he, too, at the age of fourteen, was forced to become an apprentice draper. His apprenticeship, which began in 1881, was at Hide's Drapery Emporium on the corner of what is now St Paul's Road and King's Road in Southsea. In his later autobiographical writings, Wells wrote, 'I expressed dissent, but my mother wept and entreated. I promised to be a good boy and try', conveying his 'small portmanteau to Southsea with a sinking heart'. For him, the most unendurable thing about it was that he was never master of his own thoughts, having to be continually thinking 'about pins and paper and packages'. He remained there for two miserable years before persuading his mother to release him from his indentures. In September 1883 he took up an appointment at Midhurst Grammar School as a student-teacher.

L

Levy, Benjamin

Seamen serving on board warships during the eighteenth century were rarely given shore leave for fear that they would abscond. Many, for instance, may have been forced into the service by impressment, caught by the impress gang and taken on board a naval warship desperately in need of a crew that might not return to Portsmouth for many years. This is where Benjamin Levy comes into play, usually reckoned to be the founder of a vibrant community of Jewish merchants during the early 1740s. He was an itinerant trader who set up business on the corner of Union and Queen Street, with members of that community taking small boats into the harbour, bringing their wares onto warships to trade with those on board not permitted shore leave. On 10 February 1758, tragedy struck one such group of traders, for in returning from the 60-gun *Lancaster*, a sudden squall overturned their boat, with eleven out of twenty of their number drowned. A further service offered by the Jewish trading community was the redeeming of tickets paid to seamen returning to Portsmouth after long years at sea. On being discharged, naval ratings were frequently paid their wages or prize money owed them not in cash but in tickets that then had to be taken to the Navy Office in London to be exchanged for cash. For this reason, newly discharged seamen were rarely able to purchase everyday necessities, even less so the large amounts of alcohol for which they had a reputation for consuming. Instead, they relied upon the port's traders, often those Jewish traders, to exchange their tickets, at a discount, for cash and goods in hand. Once a sufficient number of tickets had been collected, the trader would take these to London and exchange them for the sum due upon their redemption. It was, however, a system that was open to abuse, merchants, both Jews and non-Jews, sometimes discounting tickets at very high rates, much more than the 6d in the pound established by law in 1758. This was unfortunate as it sometimes led to the stigmatising of the entire community through the acts of a few. To show their loyalty and value to Portsmouth, the Portsmouth synagogue, in 1811, which was then in White's Row, collected a considerable sum for the relief of British prisoners in France, while a few months later another sum of money was given for the relief of orphans and suffering relatives resulting from the recent loss at sea of three British warships.

'Lindy', Lindbergh Delapenha

Lindbergh Delapenha, or 'Lindy' as he was more usually known, was born in Kingston, Jamaica. He was the first black player to join Portsmouth FC, making his first appearance at Fratton Park in November 1948. An inside-right, he remained with the club until April 1950 when he joined Middlesbrough. During his two-year spell he made seven appearances, scoring one FA Cup goal. He also played in the annual Portsmouth FC v. the United Services cricket match, remembered by the *Portsmouth News* as 'a flashing, forceful bat, and capable bowler'. Since then, Portsmouth has gone on to sign many African-Caribbean and African players.

Lumps Fort

Lumps Fort lies to the east of Canoe Lake and is now the site of a popular children's attraction, the Model Village. As a defensive site, a redoubt was first built here in 1545 against a possible French invasion. In a time of further crisis, when Napoleon appeared ready to invade, a much more formidable structure was built to support a small battery of guns. At one time Lumps Fort was also provided with a semaphore device to assist in the communication of messages via a chain of semaphore stations built between the Admiralty in London and the dockyard. A further fear of a French invasion led to the construction of a much larger fort, with this built between November 1859 and October 1861. At that time the fort was armed with seventeen guns, the majority facing out to sea to cover the channel leading into the harbour. During The First World War the fort was converted into a beach defence battery armed with a pair of 6-inch anti-aircraft guns. The site was acquired by Portsmouth Corporation in 1932.

M

Manning, Olivia

One important literary figure without a blue plaque is Olivia Manning, author of the 'Balkan' and 'Levant' trilogies, novels set during and immediately before the outbreak of the Second World War and collectively known as *The Fortunes of War*. They were based on her own extraordinary experiences in travelling through wartime Europe, often only one step ahead of the Nazis. That she doesn't have a blue plaque seems all the stranger given her strong associations with Portsmouth, much greater than some of those who have been given this honour. Start with the fact that Olivia was born in Portsmouth on 2 March 1908, at her parent's home at No. 134 Laburnum Grove, North End. The doctor attending the birth was Dr Weston, the model for Dr Watson of Sherlock Holmes, allowing Olivia to later remark, 'you might say I had a literary kick-start'. A further reason for a blue plaque could well be that her novels sometimes refer to Portsmouth, if somewhat covertly. In *The Play Room*, Laburnum Grove is renamed Rowantree Avenue and North End as Camperlea. She also attended school in Portsmouth – Lynton House and Portsmouth Grammar School – before being sent by her parents to train as a typist. This was clearly not for her, as she enrolled in evening classes at the Portsmouth Municipal School of Art, which was situated behind the Town Hall (now Guildhall). Indeed, her artwork was

While there is no blue plaque in Portsmouth to Olivia Manning, her strong connections with Portsmouth offer a number of possible sights. Here, in Victoria Park, she would spend time reading books borrowed from the public library, developing ideas for her future writing.

Above: If not Victoria Park then a blue plaque to Olivia Manning could well be placed on this present-day university building, familiar to Olivia Manning as the location both of the library that she frequented and the Municipal College she attended.

Left: The house of Olivia Manning's youth in Laburnum Grove.

well received, and this might have been her eventual road to fame, especially following the exhibition of one of her paintings at an art exhibition then held each year on South Parade Pier. Indeed, up until the age of nineteen this had been Olivia's greatest desire. However, she was now determined on writing. An avid reader, borrowing frequently from the Central Library she would settle down on a bench in nearby **Victoria Park**, most often absorbed in a Lawrence, Huxley or Lewis novel. Perhaps this makes Victoria Park a candidate for a second blue plaque, to honour her connection with Portsmouth. It was in Portsmouth that Olivia also began her writing career, completing several short stories and her first few novels. In search of broader horizons, she left Portsmouth during the 1930s and eventually found her way to pre-war Romania and the inspiration that gave rise to the first novel in *The Fortunes of War* series.

Mary Rose

Alongside Portsmouth's *Victory* and Stockholm's *Vasa*, the *Mary Rose* is one of the most famous and most visited of preserved ships in the world. Each year, touching on half a million come to view the *Mary Rose*, Henry VIII's flagship that sank in the Solent on 19 July 1545 when attempting to counter a French invasion fleet. The wreck was raised by the Mary Rose Trust in 1982, and subsequently went on display in a specially designed hall within the **Historic Dockyard** at Portsmouth and close-by *Victory*. Initially the *Mary Rose* was viewed through a thin film of spray formed of chilled and recycled freshwater, this necessary to keep her timbers from drying out too quickly with the water spray gradually changed to polyethylene glycol, a wax used to seal the outer layers of timber. Now, however, there is no thin film of spray. The hull is now dried out in environmentally controlled conditions and is clearly visible in a £35m purpose-built new museum that was first opened to the public in 2013.

Mill Pond

Mill Pond was the name once given to a tidal pond, which was fed from a creek that is now covered over by **Gunwharf Quays**. King's mill, used to provide flour for military and naval use, was located alongside the pond. Filling in of the Mill Pond during the late nineteenth century allowed both for an expansion of the area occupied by the Gunwharf and facilitated the building of the rail line to the harbour which ran over the one-time north bank of the Mill Pond. As for the old mouth of the creek, this had been reshaped on the building of the Gunwharf and eventually given the name Vernon Creek.

Model Village

A popular attraction for children that was created in 1956, the model village overlooks **Canoe Lake** and stands on the site of the now demolished **Lumps Fort**.

National Museum of the Royal Navy

The National Museum of the Royal Navy is the name now given to the combined museums of the Royal Navy and includes the **Historic Dockyard** at Portsmouth, within which is the National Museum of the Royal Navy, Portsmouth, formerly the Royal Naval Museum. Originally founded in 1911 as the Dockyard Museum, the Museum of the Royal Navy, Portsmouth, is home to an important collection that tells the history of the Royal Navy and is housed in former eighteenth-century storehouses immediately facing *Victory*.

The original museum, a collection of various artefacts associated with the Royal Navy and the dockyard, as established in 1911.

Nelson

Throughout the city of Portsmouth the name of Nelson abounds. On Portsdown Hill is a memorial to Nelson, this next to the fort that is named after him. The naval base also carries his name, and within the **National Museum of the Royal Navy** is the Nelson gallery, this a stone's throw from his former flagship *Victory*. Elsewhere in Portsmouth, the connection with Nelson is evident in a statue near the Square Tower, in road names, and in the names of a school and numerous commercial organisations including bars, pubs and hotels. Horatio Nelson visited Portsmouth on numerous occasions, this to either join or leave a ship to which the Admiralty had appointed him. His first appearance in Portsmouth was as a boy of seventeen when joining the 64-gun third-rate *Worcester* in October 1776 as a newly appointed acting lieutenant. Undoubtedly though, it is his last visit to Portsmouth that is best remembered, this only five weeks before his death at the hands of a sharpshooter at the Battle of Trafalgar. On that occasion, now a vice-admiral and a peer of the realm, he arrived in the town early in the morning, having travelled overnight, entering the town on a post-chaise that took him through Landport Gate. Breakfasting at the **George Hotel** in the High Street, he then paid a brief courtesy visit to the resident commissioner of the dockyard, Captain Charles Saxton, before returning to the George Hotel. Nelson, of course, was a celebrity. His naval victories at Abū Qīr Bay (1798) and Copenhagen (1801) had made him a household name, with crowds quickly assembling once his presence in Portsmouth was known. For this reason, to avoid the mêlée, he left the hotel by a back entrance, walking along Penny Street into Green Row (now Pembroke Street). Of course, he was soon spotted, with one writer describing his admirers kneeling before him and giving their blessings as he passed. It was from the beach at Southsea that he boarded the barge that took him out to *Victory* – it is now generally assumed that he would have walked past the **Garrison church** and through the tunnel cut through

Vice-Admiral Horatio Nelson, a British hero and a frequent visitor to Portsmouth.

the King's Bastion to reach the beach at a point close to the present-day funfair. On stepping onto the barge he was given three loud cheers. Three months later, with the combined French and Spanish fleet defeated, *Victory* returned to Portsmouth, this time with the body of Nelson preserved in a cask of brandy, and soon to be taken to Greenwich to lie in state prior to a funeral that accompanied a period of national mourning.

Left: The memory of Nelson in Portsmouth, through various memorials and the general use of his name, is alive and well. Among them is his statue in Grand Parade.

Below: Nelson, met by an enthusiastic crowd, boards a barge on Southsea beach that will take him to *Victory*.

O

Old Beneficial School

Situated in Kent Street, the Beneficial School building was constructed in 1784 and it was here, in 1812, that Elizabeth Dickens went into labour, giving birth to her author son, Charles. The school provided the children of the poor with an education, which was made possible through an annual subscription scheme paid by members. Claimed as the most haunted building in Portsmouth, today the Old Benny, with resident ghosts 'George' and 'Emily', is the home to one of Portsmouth's **theatres**, Groundlings.

Below left: The Beneficial School in Kent Street and now Groundlings Theatre.

Below right: Here in the High Street, George Villiers, the first Duke of Buckingham, was murdered in August 1628.

IN
THIS HOUSE
GEORGE VILLIERS
DUKE OF BUCKINGHAM
WAS ASSASSINATED BY
JOHN FELTON
23. AUG. 1628.

The plaque that records the event of the duke's murder.

Old Portsmouth

Old Portsmouth is the area of the original medieval town of Portsmouth situated on the south-west corner of **Portsea** Island. Here are many early buildings, but it was also an area that suffered heavily from bombing during the Second World War, resulting in the destruction of several buildings that would today be of significance. The midsection of the High Street is particularly attractive, with the cathedral church of St Thomas towards the south. But to the north it is a little austere due to the rather overbearing façade of the former Cambridge Barracks, now Portsmouth Grammar School. A building of note is the house, once a public house, where George Villiers, the first Duke of Buckingham, was murdered on 23 August 1628 while the **John Pounds Memorial Church** and workshop should not be missed. Also within the area of Old Portsmouth are the **Royal Garrison Church**, the **Camber docks** and the Square and Round Towers.

Ordzhonikidze

Ordzhonikidze was a Sverdlov-class cruiser of the Soviet navy that brought to Portsmouth in 1956 the Soviet leaders Nikita Khrushchev and Nikolai Bulganin on a diplomatic mission to Britain. While the ship was moored in the harbour, *Ordzhonikidze*'s hull was covertly inspected by several British divers working on behalf of both the Admiralty and MI6. Previously Prime Minister Anthony Eden had given instructions that no such survey of the Soviet ship should be made, with his instructions apparently disobeyed. Seemingly the Soviet navy was prepared to defend the underwater secrets of the ship, a bow propeller that provided the ship with additional thrust, by placing around her their own frogmen, who were prepared to intercept any British divers. Lionel 'Buster' Crabbe, an experienced but now retired British naval frogman, had been recruited by MI6 to investigate the *Ordzhonikidze* hull, disappearing after making a dive into Portsmouth

Harbour on the evening of 19 April 1956. It can only be surmised as to his fate, but the washing up of a headless body on Thorney Island several months later offered a possible clue. Alternatively, two divers working for the Admiralty also attempted an underwater survey of *Ordzhonikidze*, with one of these divers also not returning –the Admiralty failed to admit this due to the constraints placed on them by Prime Minister Eden. This raises the alternative possibility of the headless body being one of the naval divers. While an inquest on the headless body, carried out in Chichester, did officially declare it to be that of 'Buster' Crabbe, there were inconsistencies in the evidence given and the possibility of an MI6 cover-up.

Owen, Thomas Ellis

A much-revered architect in Southsea, Thomas Ellis Owen designed an estimated seventy-five villas and fifty-four terraced houses during the early to mid-Victorian years. His connection with Portsmouth began when working alongside his father, the Clerk of Works and later Chief Engineer of the Portsmouth Royal Engineers, on the structure of several local churches. The Kent Road area provides one of the greatest concentration of Owen-designed houses, these having an Italianate influence while reflecting a desire to break the monotony of regimented rows of houses – his houses were often placed in angled positions and made good use of curving avenues. Owen also contributed to Portsmouth life in other ways. He was elected to the **Corporation** and held the position of mayor on two occasions.

A typical Thomas Ellis Owen Southsea house.

Palmerston Follies

'Palmerston Follies' is the name sometimes given to the series of fortifications built to defend Portsea Island and its naval dockyard and which run along the top of Portsdown Hill. There are several possible reasons for this accolade, with Lord Palmerston, prime minister at the time of their inception in the 1860s, very much an advocate for their construction. One possibility is that with concern existing at a build-up of the French navy under Napoleon III, the forts faced the wrong way, projecting their guns to defend Portsmouth from the land rather than sea. More convincing is that by the time of their completion, they were obsolete, advances in gunnery ensuring that these forts would be no barrier to a determined attack, whether coming by land or sea.

Also accorded the title 'Palmerston Follies' are the four Solent forts – Horse Sand, No Man's Land, St Helen's and Spitbank – that were built between 1865 and 1880 for the protection of Portsmouth and its harbour from sea attack.

Piers

South Parade and Clarence Pier were both originally designed to allow passengers to board steamers for the Isle of Wight. South Parade Pier was officially opened in 1879, having been built at a cost of £89,000. Following a fire in 1904, the pier was rebuilt at a cost of £85,000 and reopened four years later. With a length of 600 feet, it possessed a spacious pavilion containing two halls, one a 1,200-seat theatre and the other a café during the day and a dance hall at night. At the seaward end there was a separate pavilion with a bar and lounge. Fires have rather haunted the pier; the theatre was lost following a fire in 1966 and a further conflagration struck in 1974, this last during the filming of *Tommy*, which forced a £500,000 rebuild.

Clarence Pier was originally opened in 1861 for steamers crossing over to Ryde, but it lacked the length of South Parade Pier. Destroyed by enemy bombing on the night of 10 January 1941, Clarence Pier was rebuilt to its present design after the war and reopened in 1961.

South Parade Pier in a late 1950s illustration highlighting the summertime experience to be gained from a visit to the pier.

Despite a serious fire in 1974 when the pier was used as a backdrop for *Tommy*, a film based on The Who's rock opera, South Parade Pier today is outwardly little different to its appearance some fifty years earlier.

Play up Pompey

A chant sung by supporters of Portsmouth Football Club. The team was founded in 1898 with their ground at Fratton Park. The chant 'Play up Pompey, Pompey play up' is sung to the tune of 'Westminster Chimes'.

Portsdown Hill

Providing outstanding views over Portsmouth and to the Isle of Wight beyond, this chalk ridge to the north of Portsmouth is both an important nature reserve and a military heritage area. The chalk grassland has been designated a Site of Special Scientific Interest (SSSI), rich in wild flowers, insects and birdlife. It is along the line of this ridge that the Victorian military fortifications, sometimes referred to as **Palmerston Follies**, are located – a line of six forts. Built because of recommendations made by the Royal Commission on the Defence of the United Kingdom, a committee formed in 1859, the forts from east to west are Purbrook, Widley, Southwick, Nelson, Wallington and Fareham. Fort Nelson, a Grade I-listed building, is now the site of the Royal Armouries, an ordnance museum. Fort Widley is owned by Portsmouth City Council. All the other forts, or what remains of them, are in private ownership. Forts Purbrook and Widley are both activity centres in the ownership of the Peter Ashley Activity Centres Trust.

Portsea

Portsea can refer to the island of Portsea, all the area south of Portsbridge Creek that separates Portsea Island from the mainland. Alternatively, it can refer to the parish of Portsea, which occupies much of the south-west part of Portsea Island and included, at one time, the distinct and separately fortified town of Portsea, which lay between the town of Portsmouth (**Old Portsmouth**) and the nearby **royal dockyard**. Portsea town began to develop at the end of the seventeenth century to provide housing for those employed in the dockyard.

Portsmouth Harbour

A large natural harbour leading into the Solent, the harbour has, for over 500 years, been extensively used by the Royal Navy as a safe and deep natural area of water for mooring warships. During previous centuries, the harbour would have been crowded with vessels, many ships of the Royal Navy held here in times of peace and in semi-readiness for any future outbreak of war. At times, ships no longer required for naval service might be converted into a floating hulk, this through a process of removing its rigging and internal equipment, and used instead to accommodate pressed seamen (before they joined a seagoing warship), prisoners of war or convicts. It was the value of this harbour as a place for warships that directly led both to the establishment and subsequent growth of the **royal dockyard.** Nevertheless, the harbour was not without problems, especially during the eighteenth century when repeated surveys showed that the mooring points for ships were becoming increasingly silted and might one day be lost to larger warships. During times of flooding, the narrow rivers that fed into the harbour, having passed through soft and muddy soil, deposited much of this into the harbour with the result that, in 1716, the area immediately beyond the dockyard possessed a depth of 26 feet, but by 1773 this had been reduced to 24 feet. An even greater problem was the sandbar that existed at the entry point of the harbour and which forced larger vessels to have their ordnance and stores removed before coming into harbour while helping trap alluvial deposits within the harbour. So serious was the problem that it threatened the value of the dockyard, for while the harbour was dredged, the hand dredgers of the eighteenth century were ineffective. Fortunately, the new century brought with it an amazing invention: the steam bucket dredger, which could shift silt from the bottom of the harbour at a rate sufficient to maintain the necessary depth for warships. More recently, the harbour has had to be dredged to an even greater depth, this permitting the new 'Queen Elizabeth'- class aircraft carriers to access the harbour, the Defence Infrastructure Organisation (DIO) awarding, in 2015, a £31 million contract to Boskalis Westminster to undertake this work.

Portsmouth Harbour from an early twentieth-century map.

The harbour, as painted by Edward William Cooke during the early nineteenth century and showing a hulk used for masting and rigging warships alongside a naval frigate.

A Wightlink ferry making a night-time entry into the harbour.

Portsmouth Point

Situated on the south side of the entrance to Portsmouth Harbour, the area was once outside the boundaries of the town with the only land approach through King James' Gate (see **Town Gates**). A highly congested area, it was a centre of maritime commerce through bordering with the **Camber**, a convenient stretch of water used for the unloading of goods brought in by ship and bound either for Portsmouth or further inland. In being outside the city walls and not bound by the bylaws of the city, the area gained a considerable reputation for drunkenness and debauchery – every fifth building at one time was a public house. Seamen were particularly attracted to the Point, as were those involved in the sex trade.

Spice Island.

Q

Q-sites

To confuse German bombers during the Second World War, potential targets such as large cities and military installations were provided with nearby decoy sites that were intended to replicate the intended target, with bombers tricked into unloading their bombs on an area away from their nominated target. Portsmouth, with its important royal dockyard, was very much a wartime target. Decoy sites to lure bombs away from

The Q-site shelter control on Langstone Harbour.

At Sinah Common on Hayling Island a further Q-site was established to lure bombers away from Portsmouth. Here, too, was a radar-equipped Heavy Anti-Aircraft (HAA) gun battery that received a direct hit from a German bomb that had the dockyard as its target. The gun emplacements that formed the HAA battery remain, the one seen here having a memorial (just visible) to those who died defending the dockyard when that bomb exploded.

Portsmouth were created at the head of Langstone Harbour and on Hayling Island. While not always successful – Portsmouth suffered badly from bombing during the war – some 200 bombs on the night of 17/18 April 1941 did fall into Langstone Harbour and Farlington Marshes instead of the more densely packed areas of Portsmouth.

'Queen Elizabeth' Class – the New Aircraft Carriers

Queen Elizabeth and *Prince of Wales* are the Royal Navy's new aircraft carriers, both to be based at Portsmouth where facilities have been created for their support. The combined cost of these two ships, of which sections have been built by BAE Systems at Portsmouth, comes at the not inconsiderable sum of £6 billion. So, what does the United Kingdom get for its money? First, both vessels, from the very outset, have been built to operate thirty-six Lockheed F-35B Lightning vertical take-off strike fighters but with the additional flexibility to allow for a mixed operation of other aircraft and helicopters, including the giant RAF Boeing Chinook helicopters. In terms of future deployment operations, the carriers are designed for heading off future potential crises, whether an armed conflict or humanitarian, able to respond to the needs of those affected, or about to be affected, by an earthquake, volcano eruption or similar. These ships are the largest ever built for the Royal Navy, each having a displacement of 65,000 tons, measuring 56 metres from the keel to the masthead with overall lengths of 280 metres. To put it another way, each vessel exhibits a paintwork area of 3,470 acres. As for the hangars below the flight deck, these are as large as twelve Olympic-size swimming pools, with the fight deck above covering 4 acres. An unusual feature is that of the flight deck having

The aircraft carrier *Queen Elizabeth* making her first entrance into Portsmouth Harbour on the morning of 16 August 2017. (Courtesy of Maria Murphy)

Above: The arrival of the new aircraft carrier was a major event for Portsmouth with thousands lining the seafront to view *Queen Elizabeth*. (Courtesy of Maria Murphy)

Below: *Dragon*, seen here berthed alongside the naval base in Portsmouth Harbour. A Type 45 air defence destroyer, she will form part of the Carrier Support Group (CSG) when *Queen Elizabeth* or her sister carrier, *Prince of Wales*, are put to sea in an operational role.

two islands, the forward one directed towards navigating the ship and the aft for flying operations. This has several advantages: the aft island is better situated to monitor the approach of aircraft; the positioning of the two in-line reduces the airflow over the flight deck. When operating at sea, the carriers will frequently operate as part of a larger carrier strike group, this made up of both escort and support vessels, although the exact mix has yet to be determined. The escort vessels will be Type 23 frigates, operating in an anti-submarine role with Type 45 destroyers in the anti-air warfare role.

R

Rock Garden

A sunken garden on the seafront at Southsea, the Rock Garden was created in 1928 with the dual purpose of providing an additional attraction for residents and visitors to Southsea and of creating work under a government-supported work scheme. In doing so, a hitherto undeveloped area of shingle was transformed, turning it into an attractive sheltered area of quiet seclusion.

Rose Garden

A 'great place to walk and enjoy these beautiful well-maintained gardens' is one visitor's comment on the Rose Garden situated in Southsea just to the east of Canoe Lake and overlooked by the Model Village. Laid out with a considerable variety of roses, it is best seen from May onwards. One unusual fact about the Rose Gardens is that it was created within the shadow of the now dismantled Lumps Fort and contains a memorial to the **Cockleshell Heroes**.

Round Tower

Originally built during the second decade of the fifteenth century, the Round Tower was intended to defend the entrance to **Portsmouth Harbour** from attack by enemy

A seaward view of the Round Tower and as it would have been seen by any approaching enemy. Immediately beyond can be seen the masts of *Warrior* and *Victory*, two of the ships on display in the Historic Dockyard. Towards the centre is the studio built by the artist W. L. **Wyllie**.

ships. Rebuilt during the reign of Elizabeth I, it was considerably strengthened during the period of the Napoleonic Wars. Today, the top of the tower is the ideal spot for viewing ships entering and leaving the harbour while the tower itself is occasionally used for events including art exhibitions.

Royal Dockyard

The royal dockyard at Portsmouth was first established on its present site during the reign of Henry VII. It remained a royal dockyard until 1984 when it was officially retitled a Fleet Maintenance and Repair Base, but is now known as HM Naval Base Portsmouth. When originally created, Henry VII's royal dockyard, the first of many royal dockyards that were to be established over the following centuries, was formed of only a few basic facilities that included a primitive dry dock, storehouses and a few workshops. Today, nothing of that early period remains, with the large pond of water to the stern of HMS *Victory*, and once known as the Great Basin but subsequently renamed the No. 1 Basin, created at the end of the seventeenth century. The Great Basin was the dominant feature of a northward extension of the yard, built between 1691 and 1698, on reclaimed marshland. Further extensions were to be added in later years, the largest of which was carried out during the late nineteenth century to provide the facilities necessary to construct iron-hulled warships and which later proved essential for the building of the revolutionary 'dreadnought' battleships of the early twentieth century. This was the 'Great Extension', a massive project that encompassed an area of 180 acres created through pushing out even further to the north. Originally centred around three new basins, several new dry docks and a series of advanced workshops, these were fundamentally completed during the 1880s.

The dockyard seen here at the beginning of the twentieth century, a destroyer entering one of the dry docks.

More recently the area of the former dockyard has seen further dramatic changes, mostly in the area around the Middle Jetty in preparation for the 'Queen Elizabeth'-class aircraft carriers.

Royal Garrison Church

That this church, close to the seafront and not far from the Square Tower, lacks a roof to the nave is a result of being left as a memorial to the air raids that struck Portsmouth during the Second World War. The church was hit by incendiary bombs and a single high-explosive bomb on 10 January 1941. The chancel, though, escaped any real damage, with this area of the church still in use. Known as the Garrison church, it was where regiments assigned to Portsmouth would attend services, with military parades in and around the area of the church a regular occurrence from the mid-eighteenth century onwards. The church, however, dates to the thirteenth century, originally part of the hospital of St Nicholas, which was established in 1212 to minister to the spiritual and temporal needs of the sick, suffering and poor. Catherine of Braganza was married to Charles II here in 1662, after having been welcomed to this country from Portugal. Ten years later James II visited the church, and in 1773 George III attended service there when he came to welcome Lord Howe following his victory on the Glorious first of June.

The Royal Garrison Church.

S

Saluting Platform

Originally a gun battery dating to *c.* 1522 and part of the harbour entrance defences, it was given over to ceremonial use in much later times, soldiers responsible for manning a gun that was fired as a salute to naval vessels entering the harbour.

The old Saluting Platform, once used for the firing of guns to salute entry into the harbour of warships and royalty.

Semaphore

A system of quickly communicating short messages between the Admiralty in London and the navy at Portsmouth was developed using a chain of semaphore stations that could signal a very basic and short message – such as a simple time check at noon – across the entire distance in less than five minutes. A more detailed message took longer as the stations, each of which was established on a high point on the route from London and within sight of another station either side, had to first record the message to be relayed and then pass the same message to the next station. The last of those semaphore stations was in Portsmouth. From 1822 until 1833 the Portsmouth station was situated on top of the Square Tower, which had a structure providing additional height built upon it. The square tower semaphore was retained as a stand-by when a new semaphore was erected on the tower of the sail loft and rigging house in the dockyard, this becoming the chief naval semaphore centre until the line was abandoned in December 1847. Due to smoke from chimneys in Portsmouth interfering with communications semaphored from **Portsdown Hill**, an additional station was created on the east side of Portsea Island, at **Lumps Fort**, so avoiding the smoke that hung over **Portsea**, with messages then relayed to the Square Tower.

Shute, Neville

Neville Shute Norway, who wrote under the name of Neville Shute, was a popular novelist writing during the early to middle years of the twentieth century. An aeronautical engineer, Neville Shute both lived and worked in Portsmouth, moving here with Airspeed Ltd, the company which he had co-founded, when relocated to the airport alongside Eastern Road in March 1933. It was at that time he acquired a house in Portsmouth, No. 14 Helena Road, continuing to live there until 1940. The house is marked with a blue plaque. While living in Helena Road he wrote several of his novels, including *Landfall*, the story of an RAF Coastal Command pilot based at nearby Thorney Island and who frequently visited Portsmouth. It is a story set during the first few months of the Second World War, with the pilot falling foul of the Admiralty for an action for which he is wrongly accused. *Landfall* was later turned into a film, which is frequently shown on British television. An earlier Neville Shute novel, *So Disdained*, also features Portsmouth. Published in 1926, it is a carefully crafted account of a former RFC pilot paid by a foreign power to take aerial photographs of the dockyard. His aeroplane is a highly advanced machine with a silenced engine that allows him to approach the harbour without giving an alert to the authorities. These are not the only books that refer to Portsmouth, as characters in many of his other novels have connections with the city through either having been born here or visiting as part of the plot line. Both Neville Shute Road and Norway Road on the former site of the airport are named after him, while Marazan Road is also in Portsmouth, this a title of a further novel, one in which the central character is the son of a naval officer and a Portsmouth chorus girl.

The former home in Helena Road of the author Neville Shute during the time he lived in Portsmouth.

Southsea Castle

Southsea Castle dates to the reign of Henry VIII, possibly to a design laid down by the king. It was built to defend Portsmouth against possible French attacks, with Henry VIII supposedly present at the castle on 18 July 1545 where he witnessed the sinking in the Solent of his warship *Mary Rose*. Finally completed in October of that year, the construction of the castle was partly financed by money raised from the sale of monastic buildings following England's break with Rome. Besieged during the English Civil War, the castle was captured by Parliamentary forces and shortly after served as a prison. Towards the end of the seventeenth century, **de Gomme** made certain improvements, viewing the castle as a useful addition to the defence of the dockyard as it commanded the deep-water channel where it came closest to **Portsea** Island. At this time the number of guns were increased while a sloping embankment gave better protection from seaborne cannon fire. Further improvements were made to the castle to allow it to play a part in the defence of the country should Napoleon invade, while during the First World War it was home to a searchlight battery. In 1960, finally withdrawn from military service, it was restored following purchase by Portsmouth City Council and then opened to the public. Entry is now free with a welcoming café and gift shop found within the walls.

Southsea Castle.

Spice Island

An alternative name for **Portsmouth Point**, the reason for this part of Portsmouth being sometimes known as Spice Island is unknown, but several reasons are put forward. Less convincing is a rather sarcastic reference to the unpleasant smells that emanated from the inner **Camber** at low tide, which was used as the town sewer. In total contrast, an alternative explanation is that it comes from the smell of spices that were once unloaded on the nearby town quay.

Spice Island, which has a certain atmospheric quality by night.

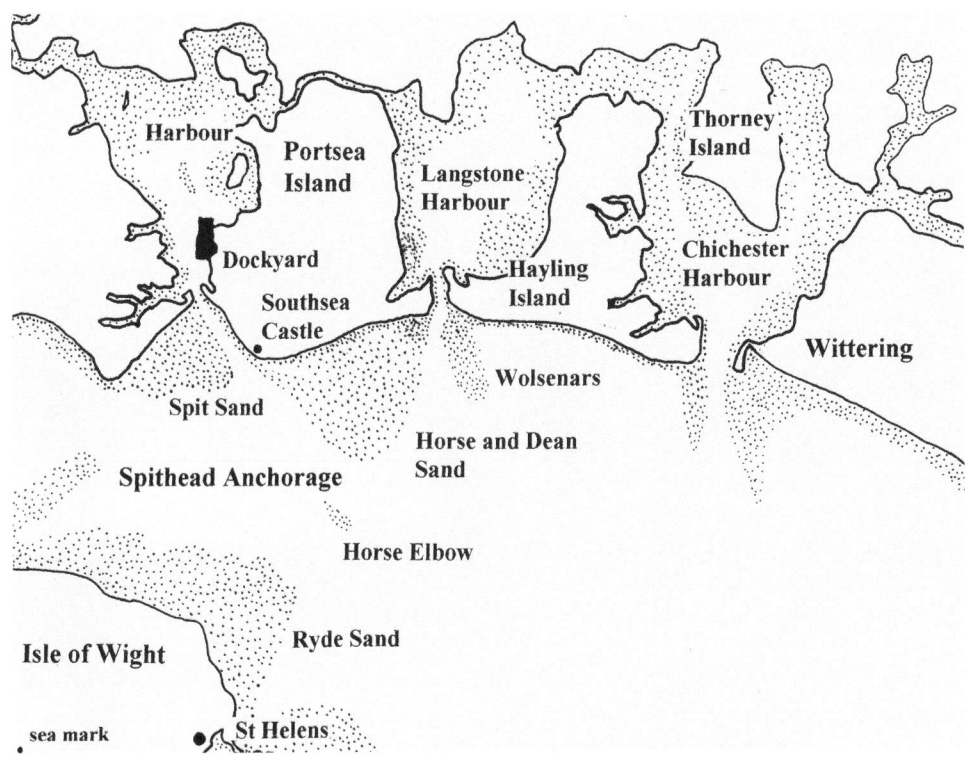

The Spithead anchorage and the position of the treacherous sandbanks that were once a serious hazard for warships entering these waters.

Spithead

An extensive and deep area of water forming the western side of the channel leading into Portsmouth harbour. At one time a major naval anchorage, it has seen, over the years, many fleet reviews in which substantial numbers of warships have been drawn together for an inspection by the reigning monarch. The last such fleet review, an international review, was held in June 2005 as part of the celebrations to commemorate the 200th anniversary of the Battle of Trafalgar. On that occasion, Elizabeth II reviewed the fleet from on board *Endurance*, the Royal Navy's Antarctic Patrol Vessel. As a gateway into Portsmouth Harbour, Spithead has not always been particularly forgiving, and during the age of sail proved quite treacherous for naval warships. Unprotected from winds to the south-east, this often made it impossible for ships to leave Portsmouth. In addition, the navigable channel that led through Spithead is partly bordered by sandbanks, one lying immediately beyond the entrance to the harbour, with Hamilton and East Sand either side of the deep-water channel. To these can be added Spit Sand and Middle Ground, providing further dangers to the north and east, respectively. Some 2 miles out from the harbour entrance were the greatest of all dangers: Horse and Dean Sands off Southsea and the extensive Warner sands off Hayling Island.

Spithead Mutiny (1797)

An important episode in naval history, crews of the Channel Fleet refused to perform duty until grievances that included rates of pay, harsh discipline, poor food and lack of shore leave had been addressed. Several months in the making, the mutiny broke out in April 1797 when crews refused to sail, this eventually spreading to over eighty ships and nearly 30,000 seamen. Conducted in a peaceful and organised manner, many of their demands were agreed with participants granted a royal pardon.

Stone Frigates

A 'stone frigate' is a naval establishment on land, the earliest of these often replacing a hulk moored in the harbour that had previously served to accommodate either seamen not living on board a seagoing warship or under training. A number of stone frigates were established in Portsmouth, and if replacing a hulk that had previously served in that role, the stone frigate retained the same name with seamen when attached to these establishments regarded as being at sea and therefore 'ashore' when not on board. Some of the larger stone frigates are listed below:

HMS *Excellent*: Located on Whale Island since the 1890s, HMS *Excellent* was the name at that time given to the Royal Navy gunnery school that had first been formed on board the hulked ship of the same name moored in Portsmouth Harbour. It is now a unit of the Maritime Warfare School and Surface Stream, with a headquarters at HMS *Collingwood* in Fareham.

Drilling sailors on the parade ground of HMS *Victory*, then the name given to the 'stone frigate' that has since been renamed HMS *Nelson*.

Not at this stage a stone frigate, this 1897 photograph shows two of the hulks, then moored in Portchester Creek, that were home to HMS *Excellent*, the Royal Navy's torpedo school which later moved to the **Gunwharf**. At that time, 1,300 men were passing through the school every year, with the vessel in the foreground the former wooden steam frigate *Ariadne*, joined end-to-end to the former 101-gun *Donegal*.

HMS *Nelson*: Opened in 1903 as HMS *Victory*, Royal Naval Barracks, Portsmouth, the barracks were renamed HMS *Nelson* on 1 Aug 1974. Of red-brick construction and to a similar design to that of barracks constructed at Chatham, many of the original buildings have been replaced. Of note, however, is the officers' wardroom in Queen Street, a building in the Jacobean style, but soon to be sold out of naval service.

HMS *Temeraire*: Currently located in Burnaby Road, this is the home of the Royal Navy's Directorate of Naval Physical Training and Sport. Commissioned as HMS *Temeraire* in 1971, this was a name once reserved for the navy's larger battleships.

HMS *Vernon*: Established at the **Gunwharf** in 1923, and specialising in torpedo and mine warfare, the name was carried over from the Royal Navy Torpedo School that had been housed since 1876 on hulks in the harbour, of which the first to perform this role had been the 50-gun *Vernon* moored in Fountain Lake.

Task Force South

It was from Portsmouth on April 5 1982 that the aircraft carriers *Invincible* and *Hermes* with escort vessels left Portsmouth for the Falkland Islands, the first ships of the Task Force. The conflict was fought over a period of eleven weeks and proved to be the most intense conflict fought by Britain since the Korean War with 130 British naval personnel killed, 257 wounded and six ships lost.

Massive celebrations met the aircraft carrier *Invincible* when she returned home to Portsmouth following the Falklands Conflict. (MoD/Crown copyright, 1982)

Theatres

Today, live drama still thrives in Portsmouth, the city having three dedicated theatres. Most recent is Groundlings in Kent Street, first opened as a theatre in 2010. The building, though, is considerably older, having begun life in 1784 as the **Old Beneficial School** but the upper floor at that time did possess a stage. The two other Portsmouth theatres were both designed from the outset as theatres and, as theatres, have a considerably longer history.

The New Theatre Royal in Guildhall Walk was opened as a new building in 1884 on the same site as the former Theatre Royal, and it integrated some structural features of the original theatre into the new design. Providing seating on four levels with a stage some 36 feet in depth, a further major change came in 1900 when Frank Matcham, the leading theatre architect of the age, was commissioned to enlarge the existing building. At this time, not only was there an increase in seating capacity, but the stage depth was increased to 65 feet, all this achieved by pushing back the theatre on land recently purchased. Given a more lavish interior décor, it was now that the theatre gained its cast-iron conservatory at the front of the building. Many famous names have appeared at the New Theatre Royal, including Ellen Terry, Marie Lloyd together (but not at the same time) as Laurel & Hardy and Morecambe & Wise. The King's Theatre in Albert Road was first opened to the public on the evening of 30 September 1907.

The King's Theatre, Albert Road.

Entrance foyer to the King's Theatre.

The New Theatre Royal in Guildhall Walk.

Many other theatres have come and gone. The Portsmouth Theatre in the High Street (**Old Portsmouth**) was the dominant venue for drama during the eighteenth century. Other theatres that once existed in Portsmouth were Prince's Theatre in Lake Road (opened as a theatre in 1872 and destroyed by bombing in August 1940); People's Palace of Variety in Lake Road; Portsmouth Hippodrome in Guildhall Walk, formerly Commercial Road (opened in 1908 and destroyed by bombing 10 January 1941); and The Empire Theatre in Edinburgh Road (opened on 31 October 1901, closed in August 1958 and demolished). Portsmouth also had variety halls and numerous other venues for stage entertainment.

Town Gates

Both **Portsea** town and **Old Portsmouth** were once surrounded by defensive walls pierced by entrance gates. For Old Portsmouth, the original gates were Landport and King James' to which the Sally Port and King William's Gate were later added, while the original gates for Portsea were Lion and Unicorn gates. Of those gates that still survive, only Landport Gate stands in its original position.

King George's Gate, situated on the east side of the **Camber** and where Gunwharf Road now meets White Hart Road, was originally known as Quay Gate as it provided entry into the town for goods unloaded on the commercial quay. Originally built 1585–94, King George's Gate was completely rebuilt in 1734.

King James' Gate was built to provide an entrance into **Old Portsmouth** from **Portsmouth Point/Spice Island.** The gate built here during the late seventeenth century replaced an earlier structure that throughout much of its time had been known as Point Gate. King James' Gate was demolished in 1878 to create a wider passage through which **horse trams** could easily pass. Partially reconstructed, it now stands in Burnaby Road alongside the United Services Recreation Ground.

King William's Gate was not built until 1834, giving an entrance through the wall into Portsmouth to the south-east and in-line with Pembroke Road.

King James' Gate in Burnaby Road.

Landport Gate, on the north-east side of Old Portsmouth, was the principal gate into the town and is the only gate that remains in its original position, albeit somewhat forlorn as an entrance into the United Services sports ground just opposite Warblington Street. Dating to *c.* 1760, it is a solid stone structure in the baroque style topped by a circular cupola.

Lion Gate, a round centrally arched stone gate built in the classical style, dates to the late eighteenth century and once provided a main access point into Portsea. It was moved in 1929 from Portsea into the dockyard to form an archway entrance onto the South Railway Jetty underneath the Semaphore Tower, at the time under reconstruction following its destruction by fire some sixteen years earlier. Designed to be used by both visiting dignitaries and those boarding ships, it was at that time renamed 'The Gate of Empire'.

Sally Port, situated between the Square and King James' Gate, was cut into the wall during the eighteenth century to provide direct access into Old Portsmouth from the Spithead anchorage.

Unicorn Gate, originally constructed *c.* 1778, once stood at the northern end of York Place but was demolished in the mid-1860s and repositioned and rebuilt to provide an attractive entrance into the dockyard.

Landport Gate.

Right: Sally Port.

Below: Unicorn Gate.

Town or City?

As to whether Portsmouth should be referred to as a town or city, this depends on the year or years to which reference is made. It was only in 1926 that Portsmouth gained the status of city, achieved on the grounds that it was the 'first naval port of the kingdom'. Before that Portsmouth possessed only town status, as did the separate parish of **Portsea**. At the time of Portsmouth gaining city status, Portsea had been administratively incorporated into Portsmouth, so also gained city status.

Trolleybuses

Replacing electric trams on most routes, trolleybuses were first introduced in 1934 but only fully replaced trams two years later. Operating a total of nine routes in the city, trolleybuses ran in Portsmouth until 27 July 1963 when they were replaced by diesel-powered motor buses.

Motor buses eventually replaced trolleybuses but were also in service on various feeder routes. Here, on display at a Southsea bus fair held during the summer of 2015, is a fully restored Portsmouth City Corporation Bedford as built in 1944.

U

Union Workhouse

The Portsea Island Workhouse was situated on St Mary's Road and built during the mid-1840s with an official opening in July 1846. Prior to 1834, both Portsmouth and **Portsea** had their own parish workhouses that were separately funded through the parish rates. The Poor Law Amendment Act of 1834 required that parishes geographically close together, if they had not already done so, should form a union for the purposes of poor relief, with an elected Board of Poor Law Guardians to govern the arrangement. Initially, the two parish workhouses, following the creation of the Portsea Island Union, that had been financed and built by the parishes of Portsmouth and Portsea to house the most destitute were retained under the new arrangement. An increase in the high number of poor brought into these former parish poorhouses following the new Act, which also discouraged paying for the poor to remain in their homes, led to the need for a much larger building. It was this that resulted in the decision to construct the Portsea Island Workhouse, a building that continued to be administered by the Board of Guardians until abolition of poor law unions by the Local Government Act of 1929. By that time, the building alongside St Mary's Road had taken on a specialist hospital role with more buildings added to the site to meet the health needs of the community. In continuing with this role after the abolition of the poor law unions, many of the original buildings have been retained with further structures added, the facility known today as St Mary's Hospital.

V

Victoria Park

With its tree-lined walkways, aviary and flower beds, this is a popular park for both residents and those who commute to Portsmouth for a lunchtime break, conveniently situated, as it is, immediately to the north-west of the **Guildhall**. First opened in May 1878, the park is especially notable for its numerous obelisks that memorialise several past naval events that have involved Portsmouth-based ships and their crews. It was also a favoured haunt of the Portsmouth-born author Olivia **Manning**.

Victoria Park.

Victory – Nelson's Flagship

Launched at Chatham in 1765, *Victory* counts as the oldest commissioned ship in the world, currently serving as flagship of the First Sea Lord, although the ship itself has, since March 2012, come into the ownership of the HMS Victory Preservation Trust, part of the **National Museum of the Royal Navy**. A tradition on each 21 October, this being the date of the Battle of Trafalgar fought in 1805, is to fly Nelson's famous signal, 'England expects that every man will do his duty.' The campaign to bring *Victory* into dry dock, and so save her for the nation, effectively began in 1910 with the formation of the Society for Nautical Research (SNR), which had, as one of its core objectives, the restoration of *Victory*. At that time, while still afloat in Portsmouth Harbour, she was in a very poor state of repair with visitors occasionally allowed on board. Brought into the No. 2 Dock in January 1922, where she has remained ever since, it was soon realised that the work required to bring her back to her 'Trafalgar' condition would require considerable financing. This was made possible through the setting up by the SNR on Trafalgar Day 1922 of the 'Save the Victory Fund' with the Portsmouth-based

Victory, Nelson's flagship at Trafalgar. (MoD/Crown copyright, 2004)

Above: A view from a 1930s photograph along the Quarterdeck of *Victory*.

Left: HMS *Victory* afloat in Portsmouth Harbour, *c.* 1900.

marine artist W. L. Wyllie a leading supporter and advocate of the cause. It was in April 1925 that sufficient work had been undertaken upon her as to allow *Victory* to be again open to the public, having now been saved for the nation. Currently, some 400,000 visit her each year, gaining a unique glimpse into the conditions of life at sea during the time when sail predominated.

W

Warrior

Warrior was the first steam-powered iron-hulled armour-plated capital ship to enter service with any navy in the world and, in her day, was the world's fastest and most powerfully armed warship. Now a major visitor attraction, *Warrior* is permanently berthed close by Victory Gate and easily visible to anyone approaching the **Historic Dockyard.** Constructed at Blackwall by the Thames Ironworks and Shipbuilding Co., and launched in December 1860, *Warrior* served much of her time in the Channel Fleet until, some ten years later, she was deemed obsolete and entered the Reserve Fleet. During the early part of the twentieth century *Warrior*, now renamed *Vernon III* and gutted of her engines and boilers, was a familiar sight in the harbour, attached

Warrior dressed for Christmas 2017.

to the Royal Navy torpedo training school as a classroom ship. Eventually in 1929, she was removed to Pembroke Dock to serve as a floating oil jetty, all her equipment and masts having, by this time, been removed. With no further use for her, *Warrior* was donated to a preservation trust in 1979 where it was decided that she should be preserved as a museum ship. Towed to Hartlepool, where she arrived in September 1979, she underwent a restoration programme at a cost of £9m, which returned her to how she had been at the time of her first commissioning.

Westermann Yarns

Percy F. Westerman, voted the most popular author of stories for boys during the 1930s, was born in Portsmouth in 1876 and eventually went on to write 174 books for children, these sometimes at the rate of four per year. Westerman still has many fans in Portsmouth, with Westerman Yarns a catalyst around which ideas and thoughts on this prolific children's author are shared. The Westerman Yarns, which collects and shares Westerman material including his books together with periodicals and annuals in which his writings appear, is very much centred on Portsmouth. Between 1880 and 1900, the future author was living with his parents at No. 55 Campbell Road and he attended the Grammar School in **Old Portsmouth**. In 1896, Westerman took up a clerical appointment at Portsmouth's **royal dockyard** and it was shortly after that his writing career began. The story is that it was the result of a sixpenny wager with his wife that he could write something better than the story he was reading to his son, who was, at that time, confined to bed with chickenpox. Percy won his bet when his first book *A Lad of Grit* was published in 1907. That son, John, for whom Westerman wrote his first book, was also to become a prolific children's author.

Winged Might, a Percy Westerman novel partly set in Portsmouth.

Percy Westerman lived here between 1880 and 1900.

Whale Island

Originally a much smaller island lying within Portsmouth Harbour, Whale Island is now much enlarged and connected to Portsea Island by a road bridge. The enlargement of Whale Island came about during the nineteenth century through the dumping of spoil taken from the dockyard during the building of new dry docks. Undeveloped and in the possession of the Admiralty, the island, during the mid-1880s, was an ideal location for the '**stone frigate**' HMS *Excellent*, the navy's gunnery school.

Wyllie, William Lionel

Often referred to as 'WL', William Lionel Wyllie, best known for his maritime paintings, was also a serial builder of studio towers onto the houses in which he lived. On 2 May 1906, Wyllie purchased a former yacht chamber and store in Tower Street. This he converted into a family home, adding a studio tower in the years immediately following the First World War to provide him with an unobstructed line of sight over the **Round Tower,** allowing him a view of the Solent. Prior to moving to Portsmouth, Wyllie had been living on the Hoo Peninsula, at Hoo Lodge, a house that overlooked the Medway. But Wyllie had found it essential to add a studio tower to the building, allowing him view of the river and the ships and boats that frequently passaged the Medway. From both tower studios he produced paintings accurately depicting the views gained once the towers had been built. Wyllie remained in Portsmouth until his death on 6 April 1931, with the renovated building and its studio becoming known as Tower House. Even before the addition of the tower to his new home in Portsmouth, Wyllie was producing evocative paintings of Britain's major warships moored in or sailing out of **Portsmouth Harbour**, these from drawings he had made while on the terrace in front of the house. Today, Tower House is marked with a blue plaque. During the 1920s Wyllie played a prominent role in the campaign to bring *Victory* into dry dock and restore the ship as a permanent memorial to Lord Nelson and the Battle of Trafalgar. Nearby, in the **National Museum of the Royal Navy**, is one of his most famous works, a panorama of the Battle of Trafalgar unveiled in 1930 by King George V. It is a carefully researched depiction of Trafalgar, painted as a gift for the campaign to save *Victory* for the nation, and shows the state of the battle at precisely 2.30 p.m. on the afternoon of the conflict. However, one inaccuracy exists: a deliberate attempt to heighten the drama of the battle scene, this the slightly later in time collapsing of the masts of the Spanish 140-gun *Nuestra Señora de la Santísima Trinidad,* once the heaviest ship in the world. The **National Museum of the Royal Navy** in the **Historic Dockyard** has, on long-term loan from the National Maritime Museum, a further work by Wyllie, an oil painting first exhibited in 1925, which depicts *Victory* in dry dock and under restoration. Elsewhere, the wardroom of HMS *Nelson* displays Wyllie's *The Glorious 1st of June* and *Copenhagen*, two important naval battles. Through these paintings and other maritime works, particularly several of his First World War action paintings, Wyllie became a much-revered national figure and one closely associated with the Royal Navy. As a mark of his importance, Wyllie was buried with full naval honours following a funeral at the cathedral, the coffin taken on a cutter towed by the Admiral's barge across the harbour, passing battleships, with their colours dipped and bugles calling, to the churchyard at Portchester where he was laid to rest.

Tower House showing the studio used by the marine artist W. L. Wyllie.

X Turret

Portsmouth, as home to the Royal Navy, has long accommodated those who serve on board naval warships, with barracks for both seamen (the **Royal Naval Barracks**) and Royal Marines (**Eastney Barracks**). Separated this way on land, the Royal Marines were also separated from seamen when on board ship, with all ships above the size of a destroyer having a detachment of Royal Marines who were required to operate one of the main guns as well as secondary armament. It was traditional for the marines to mess, or have their barracks, between the officers' quarters and wardroom aft, and the ratings mess decks forward. When it came to manning the guns of a battleship, the Royal Navy used the convention of naming the turrets by letters of the alphabet, with the two foremost turrets termed 'A' and 'B', a middle turret – if there was one – termed Q, and the rear turrets X and Y. Often it was the 'X' turret that was manned by the Royal Marines.

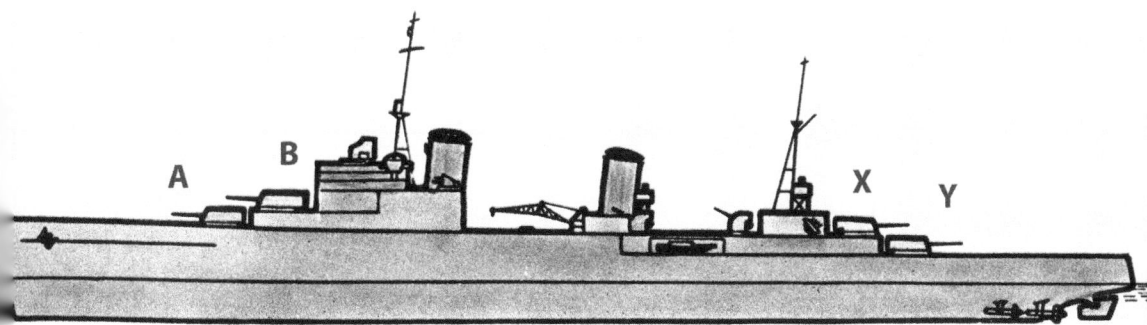

The naming of the turrets in a typical naval warship of the early twentieth century.

Yangtze Incident

HMS London is hit: 'Heavy Damage', so read the Portsmouth *Evening News* (now *The News*) on 21 April 1949. *London* was a Portsmouth-built cruiser, and this was a supposed time of peace. So, what was happening? This was all part of the 'Yangtze Incident', usually associated with HMS *Amethyst*, the ship fired upon by Chinese communist forces during the spring of 1949 as she proceeded up the Yangtze, to reach Nanking. At the time, China was in the midst of a civil war, and the communists were highly suspicious of a British warship, even one carrying a white flag as a sign of her neutrality, sailing so blatantly into Chinese territory. In passing several heavy shore batteries, *Amethyst*, on 20 April, received a considerable pounding, and was completely immobilised. To rescue her, *London*, on the following day, also came under heavy fire, retaliating with her 8-inch guns. She sustained heavy damage, with her forward 8-inch A and B turrets together with her X turret all put out of action. This forced her to retreat to Hong Kong for repairs, before being posted back to the UK. A County-class cruiser, *London* had been launched at Portsmouth on 14 September 1927, serving during the Second World War in both the Atlantic and Far East. Following a refit, *London* had again been sent out to the Far East, assigned as flagship of the fifth cruiser squadron. At the time of the Yangtze incident, *London* had been one of the most powerful ships operating in Chinese coastal waters.

How the *Evening News* presented the unfolding events in the River Yangtze.

Z

Zone of Fire

Here referred to as an open area in front of a fortification or gun battery to ensure that any attacking force will be immediately confronted by the ordnance fire of the defenders and unable to seek shelter through the zone of fire being kept completely free of obstacles, be they man-made or natural. The need in earlier times for **Portsea Island**, as one of the most heavily defended land masses in Britain, to have zones of fire for its land defences has had a considerable impact on the development of Portsmouth. Southsea Common would probably only now exist because of the military, during the early nineteenth century, requiring this area as a zone of fire for the harbour defences. When the ramparts built to defend Portsea and the dockyard from enemy attack, the development of Portsea, on the far side of those ramparts, was deliberately restricted for creating a zone of defensive fire, with the military only agreeing to houses being built here on the understanding that they would be thrown down on the landing of an enemy.

About the Author

Philip MacDougall, a former teacher at Portsmouth College, has been writing and giving talks about Portsmouth for several decades, with his initial interest focussing on the naval dockyard and its 500-year history. For Portsmouth Museums he has written *Settlers, Visitors and Asylum Seekers: Diversity in Portsmouth since the late 18th Century*, published in 2002. More recently, Philip has written *Portsmouth Dockyard Through Time* and *Historic England: Portsmouth*, both published by Amberley Publishing. Philip's next book, *Portsmouth at Work*, will be published later this year.